BLACK PEOPLE
WHO MADE
THE OLD WEST

Thousands of black men, women, and children left the South for Kansas and points west in the great "Exodus of 1879." (KANSAS STATE HISTORICAL SOCIETY, TOPEKA)

BLACK PEOPLE WHO MADE THE OLD WEST

BY

❧ William Loren Katz ❧

ILLUSTRATED WITH PHOTOGRAPHS

Africa World Press, Inc.

P.O. Box 1892
Trenton, New Jersey 08607

Africa World Press Inc.
P.O. Box 1892
Trenton, NJ 08607

Copyright © 1992, Ethrac Publications, Inc.

First Africa World Press, Inc., Edition, 1992
Second Printing, 1994

First published by Thomas Y. Crowell Company, 1977

Cover design by Ife Nii Owoo

Library of Congress Cataloging-in-Publication Data

Katz, William Loren.
　　Black people who made the Old West / by William Loren Katz:
illustrated with photographs. -- 1st Africa World Press ed.
　　　　　p.　cm
　　Adaptation of the author's The Black West.
　　Originally Published: New York: Crowell, c1977.
　　Includes bibliographical references (p.[175]-176) and index.
　　ISBN 0-86543-363-1 (HB). -- ISBN 0-86543-364-X (PB)
　　1. Afro-American pioneers --West (U.S.) --Biography. 2. Frontier and
pioneer life --West (U.S.) 3. West (U.S.)--Biography. I. Katz.
E185.925.K36　1992
978'.00496073--dc20
　　　　　　　　　　　　　　　　　　　　　　　　　92-26779
　　　　　　　　　　　　　　　　　　　　　　　　　CIP

Introduction to
the Africa World Press Edition

Black People Who Made the Old West was first published in the Summer of 1977 by T.Y. Crowell. Typical of prominent New York publishers, its publicity department sent out review copies, waited for reviews and did little else to publicize the book. Perhaps it was pleased for financial reasons that its volume remained in print for the next 13 years, perhaps it did not care. It showed no further interest after its first weeks in print.

When I left to spend that summer with friends in Seattle, Washington, I found the book had a great potential for stimulating interest among adults, particularly those interested in education. Book in hand, I was interviewed on a host of local TV and radio programs. In a 2-hour TV program arranged by a producer for the African American community, I presented pictures and data from the book to an audience of 30 children ranging in age from four to 11 who responded to my questions and information with questions with comments that were truly and unpredictably their own. In August, I was hired by the Seattle Board of education, then undertaking a bussing program, to present slide lectures to the staff hired to ride the busses and to leading school supervisors.

Since that time a vast literature has grown up around the role of African Americans in the "Old West," and well it should. The Seattle audiences, including the school supervisors I reached, had never heard of these people or their tales and were typical of white school administrators in other parts of the country I encountered in the years before and after that Summer.

Writing in the aftermath of the Los Angeles riot of 1992, it is important to say that this kind of material is needed in schools more than ever. Generations of white and black children can still proceed through a public educational system and emerge virtually unaware that "We who built this country" also means large numbers of people of color.

The men and women one meets in *Black People Who Made the Old West* are fascinating characters and many have something to say to young people of today. I have merely attempted to tell their story within the frontier setting they helped create.

No changes had to be made in the text with two exceptions. The chapter on Pompey Factor now bears a fine photograph of Factor (on page 149) that reached my hands years after the book appeared. The chapter on Edwin P. McCabe ends with some additional information about him. There is also a revised list of "Books for Further Reading" that reflects new titles which have made their appearance in the last decade.

As one who has admired and made use of its prodigious output of significant titles on African American history, I am delighted to be welcomed aboard as an author by Africa World Press. I hope its publisher, Kassahun Checole, will continue to find millions of readers of every color, young and old, in the libraries, schools and homes of this country. Such education is sorely lacking in the United States and could make an enormous difference in the way young and old will get along with one another.

William Loren Katz, 1992

Contents

Introduction

Americans have always thrilled to tales of the Old West. Frontiersmen and pioneers provided our first heroes. Today a host of novels, movies, and television shows insures the hold and influence the western experience still has on our lives and on our view of ourselves as a people.

That is why the story of the West is so important for us to understand—not as a myth but as it really happened. But it is not easy, for fantasies and folk myths have replaced the truth. This book is an effort to straighten out one phase of our national past by focusing on the part black people had in settling the frontier West.

From the time of Columbus, and some authorities believe before, black men and women helped shape the frontier. They rode with Ponce de León, Chief Osceola, Davy Crockett, Billy the Kid, Buffalo Bill, General George Custer, Bat Masterson, and Tom Mix. They explored the wilderness, trapped furs, discovered mountain passes, founded settlements, prospected for gold or silver, tended herds, fought—and joined—the Indians, enlisted in United States infantry and cavalry regiments, drifted into outlaw bands, appeared on "Wanted" lists, became sheriffs, chefs, and chiefs of Indian tribes. Most, like the white and red people they encountered in the West, were simple, hard-working average folk; some made outstanding contributions. A few went not to live by the law but to break it.

As the history of the West became the leading American folk

tale, blacks were dropped from its pages. Historians did not want black men and women included in this glorious saga, and assumed that neither did their readers. Yet the activities and accomplishments of blacks wind through the many historical records: newspapers, government reports, military rosters, pioneer memoirs, artists' sketches (and later photographs), and folk stories. A recent study reveals that more than a fifth of the cowboys who drove cattle up the Chisholm Trail were black. Another study informs us that a fifth of the blue-coated cavalrymen assigned to patrol the frontier West after the Civil War were the black troopers of the daring Ninth and Tenth Cavalry Regiments.

For purposes of this volume the West really means the frontier lands. The frontier was not always out west. In colonial times Vermont in New England was frontier land, and so was Florida southeast of Georgia. When people headed "west," they were moving toward areas not settled by many Europeans; they called these lands the frontier.

Without the black story, a true picture of the West is incomplete. Black participation is no campfire yarn, spun from frontier myths, half truths, and imagination. These men and women were a real part of life's western fabric. Their experience provides new insight into our national heritage, and illuminates the kind of people who made this land.

W. L. K.

THE EXPLORERS OF A NEW CONTINENT

ESTEVANICO

He Opened Up
the Southwest

Three great races—red, white, and black—met one another on the soil of the New World. The first black man whose name appears in the records of the New World, Estevanico, was an African enslaved by Spanish conquistadores. Yet he won the confidence of the red and white people he worked among, and opened vast portions of the continent to exploration.

Although he was sometimes called "Little Stephen" (English for "Estevanico"), some have assumed this was a humorous way of saying he was a tall or large man. There is no disagreement that he was an African, learned new languages easily, and quickly made friends across racial lines.

Born in Azamore, Morocco, around 1500, Estevanico was destined to lead a life of daring adventures and then, at the height of his success, vanish mysteriously from the scene. Before his disappearance (or sudden death, as most historians assert), he left his mark on the New World as the first man from the Old World to enter and explore parts of Arizona and New Mexico.

On June 17, 1527, Andres Dorantes and his African slave, whom he called Stephen Dorantes, boarded a ship at Sanlúcar de Barrameda, Spain, and sailed to the Americas. By then Spain's soldiers had smashed empires, seized riches, and installed Christianity in the continents across the Atlantic.

For this they needed ever more manpower. Blacks were captured in Africa and shipped across the Atlantic to fill this need. Each Spanish expedition had its complement of Africans to do the heavy work. In 1513 Balboa's men, including thirty Africans, hacked their way through the lush jungle of Panama to reach the Pacific. Then these slaves built the first ship ever constructed on that seacoast. A half dozen years later Cortez fought his way into Mexico with three hundred Africans dragging the cannons he used to terrorize the Aztecs. Other Africans assisted Ponce de León in Florida and Pizarro in Peru.

Once regions had been seized and people subdued, the Spaniards established settlements. Their African slaves became important labor in cultivating the soil, building towns in the wilderness and mining gold in this mineral-rich land. By the time Estevanico arrived in the New World there were ten thousand other Africans living and working for the conquistadores. Their labor was essential to the aims of the Europeans.

The introduction of Africans to the New World added a new element to the relationship between white and red men. Here, the red men found, was a black population brought by the Spaniards and yet discontented with their lot. The African slaves wanted to be free. They revolted against Spanish rule, fled their masters whenever they could, and hoped to find a life of liberty in the Americas. The letters that traveled between the king of Spain and his colonial governors in America reveal worries about black and red people uniting. One governor complained to King Ferdinand that his African slaves "fled among the Indians and taught them bad customs and never would be captured." Black and red people were learning they had a common enemy, and were beginning to form alliances against the Europeans. The people native to American soil were discovering that though the Spaniards brought the Africans, white and black people did not share a common goal, a mutual friendship, or respect for each other. Much as the whites had seized land belonging to native Americans, so had they seized the Africans' freedom, and forced them to labor without pay.

But because African labor was so vital to its imperial aims, Spain continued to bring Africans across the Atlantic and employ their labor in many ways. So it was that soon after they arrived in the New World, Andres Dorantes and his slave Stephen joined a Spanish expedition to the northern shore of the Gulf of Mexico. King Ferdinand had ordered the exploration, and his newly appointed governor of Florida, Pánfilo de Narváez, was personally to lead it. Among the five hundred men Narváez selected to accompany him, Stephen was probably not the only African.

When the expedition landed in Florida, perhaps at Sarasota Bay, to begin its work, it was likely that Stephen was no more than thirty. Every ounce of his physical and mental strength was needed for survival. From the outset the party floundered. It was poorly managed and quickly ran out of food. Starving, frightened men were made desperate by tropical rainstorms, quicksand, and wild animals. Some died; others deserted. Some ran off seeking a haven in the treacherous countryside.

The expedition regrouped at a native village to find it had dwindled from five hundred men to eighty men. But its calamities were far from over. It was stricken by disease, and soon there were only fifteen survivors. Narváez and his men named this resting place "Misfortune Island" and pushed on. There was no respite from the onslaught of disease, storms, animal attacks, and bad luck. Finally, Narváez lay dead and there were only four survivors—Andres Dorantes, two other Spaniards, and Stephen.

The four were destined to spend eight years searching for Spanish headquarters. They endured hardship, privation, and even enslavement by a tribe of natives. Finally, they managed to escape together and plunged into the wilderness heading westward along the Gulf Coast. The record of their wanderings and fight for survival was later written down by their leader, Cabeza de Vaca. In a hostile and unknown land, the four devised ways of remaining alive and healthy.

To win the aid of tribes, they acted as magic healers. Over diseased Indians, they made signs, recited prayers, and hoped their performance would win them food, water, and some useful directions. Stephen quickly took on this new role and became the most convincing of the four.

In time Stephen became the spokesman for the group, talking with tribes about directions and bartering for food and drink. With his ability to pick up languages rapidly he managed to converse with many different tribesmen. In his account, Cabeza de Vaca wrote that Stephen "was our go-between; he informed himself about the ways we wished to take, what towns there were, and the matters we desired to know."

In his conversations Stephen picked up an Indian tale. It told of a place called Cibola, the fabled "Seven Cities of Gold"—filled with breathtaking riches—which lay somewhere north of Mexico. News of this fabulous city spurred the four to greater efforts to reach Spanish headquarters. They knew how much the king would want to possess so great a prize.

In 1536, eight years after Narváez and his five hundred men had started out, the four survivors stumbled into Spanish headquarters in Mexico. After they had recovered sufficiently, the three Europeans left for Spain. They had had enough adven-

*Estevanico (far right) and three other remaining members of the
Narváez expedition barter with Indians for aid.*

ture in the New World. However, Stephen did not have that choice. Andres Dorantes sold him to Antonio de Mendoza, viceroy of New Spain. Stephen repeated the tale of Cibola. To prove its truth he produced some metal objects the natives had given him. These showed, he said, that smelting was an art practiced in Cibola.

In 1539 Governor Mendoza prepared to launch an exploring party toward Cibola. He selected Father Marcos de Niza, an Italian priest, to lead it. Stephen Dorantes was the logical choice for his guide.

Father Marcos sent Stephen ahead as the expedition's advance scout. To report progress, Father Marcos instructed him to send back crosses indicating his closeness to Cibola. The nearer he was to Cibola, the larger the crosses. With a few Indians and two greyhounds, Stephen headed northwest from Mexico in the direction he learned from the Indian tales.

To insure his success among the tribes, he again posed as a man with magical powers of healing. He also carried a large gourd decorated with a string of little bells and a red-and-white feather to symbolize peace and friendship. As his party moved northward and westward, it picked up Indian men and women. Many came bearing gifts and the African was adorned with jewelry from his native companions.

As he had agreed, Stephen sent back messengers to Father Marcos carrying crosses. Each one was larger than the last. They also reported that Stephen's party had swelled to three hundred men and women as it approached Cibola. Father Marcos ordered his men to speed up their pace, to narrow the gap between them and Stephen.

Then for a while no word came from Stephen. The missionary was uncertain whether to forge ahead or wait for further word. Finally, two wounded Indians staggered into his camp. They bore no cross and told a story of death. Stephen and his followers, approaching a village near Cibola, had been attacked. People scattered, some were captured, and others slain. They believed Stephen had been killed. "We are the only survivors," they stated.

Here the story of Stephen Dorantes ends and legend begins. Some historians maintain that as a slave, the young man saw his opportunity for freedom and just kept on going. Others say that Stephen abused Indian women and hoodwinked the men, so he was murdered. Some have held that the Indians resented a black man insisting he spoke for a white expedition, and slew him. The Zuñi tribe, whose pueblos he was approaching, long told a story about a brave black Mexican from "Everlasting Summerland" who entered their town and died.

Cibola was never found. It became the first great folk legend of the New World. But it was no myth that the courageous and able Stephen Dorantes was the first overseas explorer of Arizona and New Mexico. And his exploits led to the further exploration of the entire American Southwest.

There was something especially significant about Stephen's adventures. Though a slave, he became an explorer of uncommon skills. Though a foreigner, he managed to make friends with the Indians far better than Europeans. Though he sought a place of wealth and comfort, he opened a vast region to colonization, and then disappeared. Whether he ever found wealth or comfort himself, or merely death, may never be known.

DU SABLE

The First Settler
of Chicago

The Indians who lived around Chicago liked to tell visitors a joke. "The first white man who came to Chicago," they said, "was a black man." They meant Jean Baptiste Pointe Du Sable.

Although there is some dispute over his early life, most evidence points to his being born in Haiti in 1745 to a French father and an African woman who was his slave. Had he been born in the English colonies, he probably would have been sent into the fields to labor with other slaves. British and Americans believed that children of mixed parentage should have the status of the mother. The fathers also showed little concern for their offspring born to slave women. Luckily, Du Sable had a French father. When his mother died, his wealthy father sent the young boy to Paris for an education.

After his stay in Paris, he worked as a seaman on his father's ships. At twenty he was shipwrecked near New Orleans. Fearful that he might be enslaved because of his color, he persuaded Jesuit missionaries to hide him until he was strong enough to leave.

In 1779 he traveled in the area of the Chicago River, engaged in the business of trapping for furs. But he was now a Frenchman in a territory recently taken from France by her enemies, the British. When war again flared between the two countries, he was arrested for "treasonable intercourse with the enemy." He spoke enough English to convince his captors he was loyal to the British crown, and the charges against him were dropped.

A British report on Du Sable in 1779 shows that he lived on an outpost settled by Indians, the site of present-day Chicago. It also indicated he was thought of as "a handsome Negro, well educated." The British were convinced he had a "good character" and had "in every way behaved in a manner becoming to a man of his station." After his release, he returned to Chicago and his friends.

For sixteen years he lived at the mouth of the Chicago River. He carried on his fur-trapping business and started a family. Like many a French trader, he met a native woman named Catherine. She was a Potawatomi and their love was deep and long-lasting. He may have missed Paris life, but he had brought some of it with him to Chicago. His log cabin was decorated with twenty-three European paintings. One can only wonder what his friends Daniel Boone and Chief Pontiac thought of this unusual frontiersman.

Soon the Du Sables had a son and a daughter. Their life together was happy, and most of their friends were from Indian tribes in the area where they traded. With its central location, many red and white men stopped at the Du Sable post to trade furs and make conversation. The host provided liquor, and

Jean Baptiste Pointe Du Sable. (CHICAGO HISTORICAL SOCIETY)

grizzled trappers and hearty Indians swapped stories and boasts.

Later Du Sable purchased eight hundred acres of land in Peoria, but he always considered Chicago his home. Each year he added to his settlement. In time it grew to include a 40' x 22' log cabin, a bakehouse, a dairy, a smokehouse, a poultry house, a workshop, a stable, a barn, and a mill. Du Sable made his living trading in furs, but he was also a miller, a cooper, and a husbandman.

Later in life Du Sable and Catherine decided to formalize their marriage as Catholics. They traveled to Cahokia, and there a Catholic priest married them. Two years later their daughter, Susanne, was married, and soon afterward they became grandparents. Susanne's child became the first to be born in Chicago. Meanwhile, their son, Jean, set out on his own for Missouri and adventure.

As a well-known and respected resident of the region, Du Sable decided to run for election as chief of some neighboring tribes. Since he had many friends among the Indians, he felt it mattered little that he himself was not a native. There is no way of knowing whether he campaigned hard for the position or merely sat at home trusting to his popularity. Either way, the outcome was a grave disappointment, for he lost. He and Catherine decided it was time to pull up stakes. He sold his 30 cattle, 38 hogs, and chickens and 2 mules. He sold his land and property for $1,200 and left Chicago forever in 1800.

The Du Sables moved in with their daughter, who was now living in St. Charles. As his life drew to a close, the founder of Chicago worried about the future. He did not want to become a public charge, dependent upon the community for relief. And he did not want to be buried anywhere except in a Catholic cemetery.

With the onset of old age, he had to file bankruptcy proceedings in 1814. But his last hope was realized. When he died four years later, he was laid to rest in the St. Charles Borromeo Cemetery, a Catholic burial ground.

In the middle of Chicago's business district there is a plaque marking the location of Jean Baptiste Pointe Du Sable's cabin of 1779. Today, blacks as well as whites rush past the plaque to the high-paying jobs in the area. The old fur trapper, who died in poverty, would have found modern Chicago very different from the outpost he settled.

YORK

Explorer of the
Louisiana Territory
with Lewis and Clark

In the spring of 1804 the United States launched its most ambitious exploration in history, the Lewis and Clark expedition. On September 23, 1806, and more than eight thousand miles later, the party of forty-four arrived back in St. Louis. They had traveled through Missouri, Kansas, Nebraska, Iowa, North and South Dakota, Montana, Idaho, Washington, and Oregon—the first non-natives to explore the huge territory President Jefferson had purchased from Napoleon. This Louisiana Territory had doubled the size of the United States, but had cost only four cents an acre, a bargain similar to the purchase of Manhattan island for $24 in trinkets.

Two of the expedition's most important members were not white. Sacajawea, a Shoshone woman, was married to a French trapper who served the expedition as guide. She proved invaluable as an interpreter and emissary to the native tribes. Her contribution has been recognized in history texts, and she is represented in more statues in the United States than any other woman.

On the other hand, York, Clark's black slave, has slipped out of the pages of history. Yet he was a hard man to ignore. Over six feet in height and weighing more than two hundred pounds, he was often the main attraction for the natives who visited the explorers. Many had not seen a black man before, or at least not one so large. To the delight of visitors, York would jump and bound about, showing a remarkable athletic agility. All this he did in good humor—a form of friendly communication to those who might find his spoken language difficult to understand.

He played his role as the expedition's star attraction to the hilt. When one tribe presented a dance entertainment for the Lewis and Clark party, the leaders wondered how to reciprocate the favor. They asked York to dance, and he did, Clark noting in his diary that York "amused the crowd very much, and Somewhat astonished them, that So large a man should be active." Another time, among the Mandans in North Dakota, York patiently submitted to an examination of his skin. Tribesmen wet their fingers and rubbed his black skin to see if the color would come off. For those who had seen only white and red-skinned people, this was an important scientific experiment. The moment was preserved in a painting by the noted western artist Charles M. Russell.

When the party reached Idaho and the Nez Percé tribe, York danced and allowed them to rub his skin. Clark's diary recorded a story York concocted for the tribe: "By way of amusement he told them that he had once been a wild animal, and caught, and tamed by his master; and to convince them showed them feats of strength which, added to his looks, made him more terrible than we wished him to be." The Nez Percé were pleased with York and permitted him, along with the white

York allows the Mandan Indians to see if his black skin color will rub off.

males in the expedition, to take an "Indian wife" during their two-week stay.

Despite his comic and athletic feats, York was considered powerful medicine by those he met. He was taken seriously, and accorded the respect due a man of his skills. A Flathead tribesman recalled that his people thought York had merely painted himself in charcoal: "Those who had been brave and fearless, the victorious ones in battle, painted themselves in charcoal. So the black man, they thought, had been the bravest of his party."

As the mission across the continent progressed, York learned more frontier skills. Hunting, fishing, and swimming were required, and he excelled in each. Along with Sacajawea and her French-Canadian husband, he served as an interpreter. Messages from Indian tribes went from the Indian woman to her husband to York and then to Lewis or Clark—York had probably picked up some French during his stay in St. Louis before the expedition began. However, one member of the party felt that York "spoke bad French and worse English."

With the other members of the party, York survived the rigors of the difficult journey from St. Louis to the Columbia River and back. Indeed, he had contributed to its success in many ways—from utilizing his frontier skills to serving as an informal ambassador of good will to all he met.

According to one tale, when York returned to St. Louis, Clark freed him and he set forth into the wilderness, where he became a chief of an Indian society in the West. Unfortunately, there is no foundation to this story. Despite his enormous help to the expedition, Clark did not free his slave. York returned to bondage and an unknown future.

GARCIA

Life Among
the Florida Seminoles

During the colonial era, slaves from Georgia and other southern colonies fled to the Spanish province of Florida. Spain and England were enemies on land and sea, and each sought ways to undermine the stability of the other. Enticing slaves southward from the Carolinas and Georgia infuriated the British masters, so Spanish Florida held its doors wide open for runaways.

At St. Augustine slaves were received hospitably. Some were recruited along with Seminoles and Creeks to attack British settlements. Others served as agents for the French or Spanish, or sailed the pirate ships operating along the coast of Florida.

Few blacks sought out the Spanish once they reached Florida. Instead, most seized an opportunity to live among the Seminole tribes or in all-black communities along the river banks. The Seminoles treated the ex-slaves well, though sometimes they still considered them slaves. They donated hoes, axes, and weapons to the blacks, who repaid their kindness with ten bushels of corn a year. Out in the wilderness these black pioneers cleared trees, built houses, and raised corn. Soon cattle, hogs, and horses roamed in the settlements.

Florida increasingly became a haven for slave runaways. Hundreds, if not thousands, fled the southern states to make it their home. By the War of 1812 numerous black towns dotted the northern Florida countryside. A number of blacks continued to live among the Seminoles, who offered armed protection and economic aid to their black allies. A former slave population grew strong and free in Florida. An American surveyor described them as "gigantic in their proportions . . . the finest looking people I have ever seen!"

Black families prospered, children grew to adulthood, and livestock roamed near neat cabins. However, the men carried arms, a precaution against the constant threat of slaveholder invasions from the North. Fishermen, farmers, and hunters were always prepared for a blow aimed at their family's liberty.

During the War of 1812 "War Hawks" in Congress eyed Florida greedily. Here was a lush land poorly defended by the Spanish, just awaiting proper exploitation. Slaveholders in Congress reminded the nation that Florida was, in the words of General Andrew Jackson, "a perpetual harbor for our slaves." Florida would have been enough of a threat to the slave system had it merely been a haven for runaways. But it was more than that. The very existence of its successful black settlements refuted a major justification of black bondage—that blacks could not survive in freedom. Here were free and prosperous people, armed to defend themselves and allied with powerful native tribes.

A group calling themselves Patriots, mostly Georgians who viewed Florida with the aim of placing it under American control, began actions in 1812. They plotted to seize St. Augustine

A runaway slave in the Florida Everglades.

with United States troops and ships. American control, to the Spanish, would mean an end of their domination. To the Indians it would mean loss of their land. But to blacks it would mean the end of precious freedom. The black population of Florida consistently rallied the others against United States invasions. In July 1812, red and black warriors struck American plantations owned by Patriots, St. Augustine's blacks providing soldiers and leaders.

By 1813 Tennessee militia and United States troops had been ordered into battle against the red and black men of Florida. But despite their overwhelming numbers, resistance held them back from too rapid an advance. The Patriot leader died, ambushed by blacks. The United States had to renounce publicly its intention of capturing the Florida peninsula.

At the conclusion of the War of 1812 the British pulled back their forces and left for home. In Florida they abandoned Fort Negro, a well-fortified position in the Apalachicola River that included heavy artillery. Some three hundred black men, women, and children lived in the fort; their commander was a black man named Garcia. Historian Kenneth Wiggins Porter has described Garcia as "a lean, tense man, hot-eyed and tight-lipped, cunning, courageous and cruel." He was well suited to his time and the danger confronting his people.

Fort Negro stood as a powerful symbol of black power and lay within reach of oppressed slaves from the southern United States. Its immediate destruction became a war aim of the United States. General Andrew Jackson ordered General Edmund Gaines to destroy it "and restore the stolen negroes and property to their rightful owners." With a fleet of vessels commanded by Colonel Clinch, Creek mercenaries, and his regular United States troops, General Gaines intended to do just that.

In the summer of 1816 the United States forces stood outside Fort Negro, challenging Garcia and his band of three hundred. When Colonel Clinch called on Garcia to surrender, the black leader shouted he would sink any boat and gun down any American force that came within range. A delegation of Creek chiefs sent to bargain with Garcia was turned away. "The Black Chief heaped much abuse on the Americans," they reported back to their white commander. To make his point unmistakably clear, Garcia hoisted a red flag and a British flag and fired off his cannons.

In the early morning of July 27 the United States gunboats began their attack on Fort Negro. Cannonballs bounced harmlessly off the three strong walls of the fort or landed in the Apalachicola mud. Colonel Clinch then ordered one ball to be heated red-hot in the stove and fired. It landed inside the fort's ammunition supply.

The destruction of life and property was terrifying. Most of the hundred warriors and two hundred women and children died in the flaming roar of the explosion. Only sixty-four survived, and of these only three were uninjured. Colonel Clinch reported he and his men rushed in, but felt "compelled . . . to pause in the midst of victory, and to drop a tear for the sufferings of [our] fellow human beings, and to acknowledge that the great ruler of the Universe must have used us as an instrument in chastising the blood thirsty murderous wretches that defended the Fort."

Garcia was found uninjured. A firing squad ended his life. The other survivors were marched north to slavery in Georgia.

Black and Seminole resistance did not end that bloody July day in 1816. It continued through three Seminole wars, the most costly the United States had fought, and did not end until the 1840s. Repeated United States invasions of Florida's lands controlled by black and red warriors finally convinced Spain to sell Florida to the United States. But warfare continued. In 1836 General Thomas Jessup claimed, "This, you may be assured, is a Negro, not an Indian war." It was both: a black fight for liberty with heavy Indian support.

In the United States Congress, Representative Joshua R. Giddings denounced his government for attacking "those who had fled from oppression, who had sought asylum in the swamps and everglades of Florida, who had fled from oppression by professed Christians, and sought protection of savage barbarians. Against them the warlike energies of this mighty nation were brought to bear, for no other cause than their love of liberty."

The spirit of Garcia would live on in Florida, where the black fight for freedom was undaunted by the oppressors superior weapons and strong power. Under men such as Garcia, blacks took up arms in defense of rights and battled for generations. Some never agreed to peace, and today some of their descendants claim that Florida still belongs to the Seminoles and their black allies. Their argument is simple: "We never surrendered."

THE
FUR TRADERS

JAMES BECKWOURTH

Crow Chief
and Fur Trapper

The early fur trappers, few of whom could read or write, won an important place in American history books and the nation's folklore. Though few recorded their adventures, and those written down for them were filled with fanciful tales, their contribution has been preserved, and with good reason. Fur traders discovered more rivers and mountain passes in the West than all the government expeditions sent out for that purpose.

Trappers searching for furs and pelts charted the ways for pioneer families. This was not their purpose, for they were busy enough surviving and bargaining in the wilderness. With loads of cheap trinkets and whatever else they thought would catch the fancy of tribes they encountered, they set out hunting for the skins of the bear, buffalo, and deer and the furs of beaver, mink, otter, and fox.

They became highly specialized in the art of surviving in a hostile forest among unknown enemies, both man and beast. They knew when to be careful, when to make friends, and when to strike first. Sometimes they figured wrong and died. When they met at roundups, amid the singing, drinking and shouting, they exchanged stories of their heroism. Though these were tall tales, they also included hints or perceptions on how to survive on the frontier. Shaggy, grizzled men listened and nodded, laughed, and learned.

Throughout its history the fur trade had caused conflict and war as much as it aided exploration and business. The French and Indian War of the colonial era was for control of the fur-rich Ohio valley. After the war, the enormous profits offered by the fur trade sparked an entire western exploration. To prevent friction with the tribes of the Old Northwest, the United States Congress tried to license traders and regulate their conduct. In 1795 it tried to establish trading companies under its control to minimize conflict between white and red trappers. By 1822, however, it admitted its failure to regulate this business and pulled out of the fur trade.

By the 1850s the fur trade had become a major American industry. The American Fur Company, started by German immigrant John Jacob Astor, won a monopoly of the Great Lakes trade. This made it the largest business in America before 1850. Its methods left much to be desired. General Zachary Taylor, a future President, once characterized its agents as "the greatest scoundrels the world ever knew."

Histories of the fur trade have usually pictured an occupation dominated by French and Scotch-Irish immigrants, and indeed they played a leading part in its growth. However, blacks also played a hitherto unheralded part since the early days of the new nation. They were among the entrepreneurs, voyageurs, and hunters. Colonel James Stevenson, who spent thirty years living among and studying native tribes, in 1888 spoke of the importance of blacks: "The old fur traders always got a Negro if possible to negotiate for them with the Indians, because of their 'pacifying effect.' They could manage them better than the white men, with less friction." Scholars have confirmed this judgment by Colonel Stevenson.

It is in the above context that the fascinating career of James P. Beckwourth can be understood. A contemporary of Kit Carson, Jim Bridger, and Davy Crockett, Beckwourth matched each for heroism, hard work, and accomplishments. Yet tough, pugnacious Beckwourth has been omitted from history books, and the tales of great mountain men do not mention him.

Born in 1798 of a union between a white man and a black slave, Beckwourth began life at the bottom, probably as a slave in Virginia. At nineteen he was taken to St. Louis and apprenticed to a blacksmith for five years. Bustling St. Louis was crowded with those planning to explore the wilderness or returning from it with tales of high adventure. It was a man's town, with women in short supply, and young, pretty ones at a premium. Beckwourth soon clashed with his burly master over his desire to come and go as he wished in the evenings. The exact issue remains unclear. At any rate, Beckwourth slugged his master and fled.

He did not stop at the St. Louis city limits, but headed west. After landing a job with Colonel William Ashley's Rocky Mountain Fur Company, Beckwourth quickly set about learning frontier skills. He became an expert with the gun, bowie knife, and tomahawk, and probably with bow and arrows as well. He earned a reputation for a quick temper, his willingness to fight, and a casual acceptance of bloodshed or death. People who valued their limbs and life avoided arguing with him.

Beckwourth was an ambitious man, ever ready to turn chance into opportunity. In 1824 he was brought into a Crow village by some of the tribe. An old woman rushed up to him and claimed he was her long-lost son. "What could I do under

James Beckwourth.

the circumstances?" Beckwourth wondered. He quickly concluded, "Even if I should deny my Crow origin, they would not believe me." He accepted adoption by the Crows and began his rise to tribal leadership.

The chief presented a comely daughter to Beckwourth in marriage. Beckwourth accepted eagerly and, to assert his control, soon picked a fight with her. The chief did not miss the message: Here was a man who knew how to utilize power. Beckwourth's first Indian name was "Morning Star." When the Crows got to know him better, it became "Bloody Arm." Beckwourth led the Crows into battle against their Blackfeet enemies. He boasted, "My faithful battle-axe was red with the blood of the enemy." In time he was chosen by the chief to replace him.

Still in his twenties, Beckwourth was convinced that more awaited him than life among the Crows. After several years he left to resume his wanderings in the West. During the third Seminole War in Florida he served as an Army scout. In 1843, traveling with a Spanish wife, he encountered pathfinder John Charles Frémont sixty miles east of the Rockies. During California's revolt against Mexico, General Philip Kearny asked for his aid, saying, "You like war, and I have good use for you now." After assisting Kearny as a scout and interpreter, Beckwourth traveled throughout the western lands and prospected for gold.

In 1850 Beckwourth crossed the Sierra Nevadas. His companions were searching for gold, but he was looking for a pass through the high, rugged terrain. "Swarms of wild geese and ducks were swimming on the surface of the cool crystal stream," he reported, and "deer and antelope filled the plains."

In that unspoiled wilderness Beckwourth discovered a pass through the mountains into the American Valley. A few miles northwest of what is now Reno, Nevada, Beckwourth Pass still stands. The mountain peak, town, and valley nearby still bear his name. For a number of years a Denver street and church also carried his name.

Beckwourth led the first wagon train through his pass— seventeen wagons filled with men, women, and children crossing into California with "gold fever." A few years later he settled down in the valley named after him. He found himself "transformed into a hotel-keeper and chief of a trading post. My house is considered the emigrant's landing place, as it is the first ranch he arrives at in the golden state, and is the only house between this point and Salt Lake."

A few years later Beckwourth met with journalist T. D.

Bonner to write down his adventurous life story. Beckwourth talked and Bonner wrote, and how much of each is present in *The Life and Adventures of James P. Beckwourth* is not possible to determine. There is no mention that Beckwourth is black. On the other hand, the author advances claims for Beckwourth's feats that rank with the tallest of tales. The preface by Bonner states: "His courage is of the highest order, and probably no man ever lived who had met with more personal adventure involving danger to life."

Unquestionably, Beckwourth exaggerated the truth when it touched on his talents and powers. But this is to be expected from the frontier breed he came from. In the outdoor tradition initiated by Captain John Smith, Daniel Boone, and Davy Crockett and still carried on by American hunters and fishermen, Beckwourth made a good story better. Recent scholars have discovered, however, that Beckwourth generally told the truth on most matters dealing with known historical events.

In 1866 Beckwourth died under circumstances that have never been made entirely clear. It seems he fell ill of food poisoning on the plains, on the way to a Crow village. However, this story has given rise to a different tale and legend now holds that Beckwourth responded to a Crow invitation to a feast. The tribe had asked Beckwourth again to lead them, but he turned them down. Then, they poisoned him. If they could not keep him as a live chief, they would keep him in the village burial ground.

GEORGE BONGA

Enterprising Voyageur
in Minnesota

Most slaves labored on plantations. This fact has given rise to a myth that slaves could or did do little more than field labor. As a result of this thinking, it has been difficult for Americans to conceive of blacks except as a mass of nameless people laboring in cotton, rice, or tobacco fields. In the South during the pre–Civil War era, however, slaves were also skilled as craftsmen and artisans, and they served a variety of functions for the southern economy.

In the North and West, slaves performed a vast array of jobs. Some worked as printers or in factories, and one served as an engineer aboard an early railroad train. Many northern masters knew from personal experience that their slaves could handle responsibility and complicated tasks.

In the late eighteenth century a British officer brought a black couple named Bonga to Minnesota, where he used them in various jobs on the frontier. The couple's son Pierre, still a slave, became part of the North West Company, serving a Canadian fur trapper in the region. His master trusted Pierre with important matters, placing him and a white man in charge of the company when he had to leave on business.

Pierre began to develop his own skills in Minnesota. His facility with the Chippewa language became very useful to the fur-trapping company. For many years he was their interpreter with the tribe, negotiating several agreements. In one Chippewa village he met and married a young woman.

The couple settled down near Duluth, and in 1802 a son, George, was born. The parents managed to send their son to Montreal, where he attended school. This may have involved no small sacrifice, for every able-bodied hand was needed to help support the family on the frontier. It also indicates that by this time the Bonga family may have won its freedom.

When George Bonga returned to the Chippewas, he also chose a bride. By then he spoke English, French, Chippewa, and several other Indian languages.

His talents were in great demand, for a man who possessed frontier skills and spoke English, French, and Indian languages was most useful to an expanding United States. Governor Lewis Cass, later a presidential candidate, hired George Bonga to negotiate with tribes in the Lake Superior region. Cass was then governor of Michigan. The Chippewa treaty of 1837, and perhaps several other treaties, owed much to Bonga's efforts as interpreter and negotiator. At the formal signing at Fort Snelling outside of St. Paul, Bonga stood among the signatories to see that all went smoothly.

In the heart of the fur-trapping region of the nation, George Bonga continued to support himself by working in the trade. He was a voyageur for the American Fur Company, maintaining posts at Lac Platte, Otter Tail Lake, and Leech Lake. At

George Bonga. (MINNESOTA HISTORICAL SOCIETY)

Leech Lake he built a home to live out his later days, and became a successful independent fur trapper.

George Bonga was a local legend among both red and white men. His frontier skills, command of languages, and ability as a diplomat assured him of friends wherever he went. He was an imposing figure, a powerful, six-foot, two-hundred-pound man who, even in his old age, gave off a feeling of quiet power.

In 1856 Judge Charles E. Flandreau, after an exhausting canoe trip to the source of the Mississippi, arrived at the Leech

Lake home of George Bonga. The judge and the old trapper, whom he described as "the blackest man I ever saw," spent two weeks sharing stories of the Old Northwest. Others dropped in at Leech Lake during the judge's stay, and Bonga "would frequently paralyze his hearers when reminiscing by saying, 'Gentlemen, I assure you that John Banfil and myself were the first two white men that ever came into this country.' "

When Bonga offered to show his guest "how royally they travelled" in the American Fur Company, the judge could not turn down the offer. Bonga assembled twelve hearty Minnesota men, and in birch bark canoes, and to the singing of a French Canadian, they paddled away. Each evening Bonga related some of the tales that had made him a local hero.

At this time the slavery controversy was exploding in violence in Kansas and about to ignite the nation with civil war. But here was a black man, Judge Flandreau recalled, who had become "a prominent trader and a man of wealth and consequence." After his two-week stay was up, the judge left "this thorough gentleman in both feeling and deportment" and made his way home. Forty-two years later, when serving as associate justice on the Minnesota Supreme Court, Judge Flandreau gave the State Historical Society his recollections of George Bonga and of his place in Minnesota society. It is the only thorough record of George Bonga's contribution to his state and nation.

We do know, however, that there were many more Bongas. More than a hundred descendants survived in Minnesota, lending their name, with its spelling altered, to Bongo Township in Cass County.

THE
EARLY SETTLERS

LUCY TERRY PRINCE

Crusader in
Colonial New England

The story of Lucy Terry and her husband Abijah Prince is a romantic and largely happy one. It took place not in the colonial South but in frontier New England, where attitudes of whites toward blacks and slavery were less harsh.

Although bondage had spread to all parts of the American continent in the colonial era, slaves never numbered more than 2 percent of the population in New England. Therefore whites tended to view them as less of a threat to their power than did slaveholders in the South who owned vast armies of blacks. While their conduct was strictly controlled by white law in the North and South, blacks in New England enjoyed many more privileges.

There they were admitted to hospitals, served in the militia, had their own churches and friendship organizations, and associated easily with family members. A visitor to Connecticut in 1704 was shocked to find "slave masters too indulgent . . . to their slaves; suffering too great familiarity from them, permitting you to sit at table and eat with them (as they say to save time), and into the dish goes the black hoof as freely as the white hand."

The greatest danger faced by New England whites was from native tribes whose land they had taken, not from blacks whose labor they exploited. Perhaps this helps explain the consideration given black slaves. An alliance between blacks from within the community and Indians from outside would have spelled doom for many a white settlement. "Their mixing," warned a British officer about red and black people, "is to be prevented as much as possible."

New England Quakers frowned on slaveholding and urged people to free and educate their bondsmen for entrance into white society. While the Quakers themselves were objects of scorn and violent attacks, they became the first white group to challenge man's right to hold others in bondage.

The story of Lucy Terry and Abijah Prince unfolded as New England was moving steadily away from slavery and toward revolution against England. Captured in Africa at five, Lucy Terry was sold to a kindly Deerfield, Massachusetts, couple. At that time Deerfield sat in the middle of a no man's land at the northernmost edge of the British colonies. It was a pathway for the hostile French and their Indian allies in Canada. Deerfield lived under constant threat of attack.

In 1746 the inevitable happened. Indian warriors from the north struck at Deerfield, killing several citizens. Lucy Terry was only sixteen and may well have served as a nurse for the wounded and dying. The event made an indelible impression on her and she soon put an account of it into words. Her rhymed description of the attack, "The Bar's Fight," became the first poem by an African written on this continent. But its value lay especially in its accurate rendition of the event. It is

still considered the best description of the raid on record. This
was her story:

THE BAR'S FIGHT

August 'twas the twenty-fifth
Seventeen hundred forty-six
The Indians did in ambush lay
Some very valient men to slay
Twas nigh unto Sam Dickinson's mill,
The Indians there five men did kill
The names of whom I'll not leave out
Samuel Allen like a hero fout
And though he was so brave and bold
His face no more shall we behold
Eleazer Hawks was killed outright
Before he had time to fight
Before he did the Indians see
Was shot and killed immediately
Oliver Amsden he was slain
Which caused his friends much grief and pain
Simeon Amsden they found dead
Not many rods off from his head.
Adonijah Gillet, we do hear
Did lose his life which was so dear
John Saddler fled across the water
And so escaped the dreadful slaughter
Eunice Allen see the Indians comeing
And hoped to save herself by running
And had not her petticoats stopt her
The awful creatures had not cotched her,
And tommyhawked her on the head
And left her on the ground for dead.
Young Samuel Allen, Oh! lack-a-day
Was taken and carried to Canada

The poem, often read aloud in the town, made Lucy Terry something of a celebrity. Young people came from all around to hear her stories. In the years that followed, Lucy Terry met Abijah Prince, a slave who had served in the militia during the French and Indian War. Prince was granted his liberty, perhaps for serving faithfully in the militia. His former master presented him with three valuable parcels of land in Northfield, Massachusetts.

Abijah purchased Lucy's liberty from her owners, and in 1756 he and Lucy were married by Justice of the Peace Elijah Williams. Their early life was happy and lucky. An employer gave Abijah a one-hundred-acre farm in Guilford, Vermont. By his own application to George III and the governor of New Hampshire, Prince became one of the fifty-five original founders of the town of Sunderland, where he owned another large farm.

By standards of the time the Princes were prosperous landowners, moderately educated, and good neighbors. They worked to improve their property, aided the various towns near their lands, and regularly paid their taxes. Two of the Princes' sons served in the American Revolution, one doing so by falsely giving his age as fifteen. After the war, the Princes looked forward to the "rights of man" promised by the American Revolutionary leaders.

They were doomed to disappointment. Two years after the war ended the Prince farm at Guilford became the target of a white neighbor who wanted the land. Haystacks were set afire and fences torn down at night. Abijah, now close to eighty, was too old to do much. But Lucy, twenty-five years younger, was determined to gain justice. She mounted her horse and rode across Vermont to carry her case to the governor's council.

The council heard her plea. Though they knew her antagonist was a wealthy and influential man, they found in her favor. The neighbor was ordered to cease and desist from harming the

Prince property. Lucy Prince rode home assured that American justice had improved since the Revolution. Never before in American history had a black woman reached so high into the sources of power and achieved such success.

Her optimism proved misplaced, however, when she tried to enter her youngest son, Abijah, Jr., in the new Williams College. After all, his brothers had fought for their country with George Washington and now he wanted a decent education. She traveled to the college and spoke to the trustees. While she knew that no black person had yet entered an American college, she pointed out the family's military record and her son's thirst for knowledge. Elijah Williams, whose will had established the college, had officiated at her wedding, she told the trustees.

To further support her arguments, she quoted from the Bible and cited some laws affirming the rights of man. The trustees listened politely to her three-hour argument. They were not unimpressed by her learning and presentation. But they told her they had no intention of admitting any black person, no matter how patriotic or interested in education he was. Lucy Prince returned home to her husband and family vastly disappointed.

The Prince family continued to lead a contented life, despite their latest setback. Then, in 1794 Abijah died, leaving a vacant place in Lucy's heart. He was buried on their Guilford farm, and for eighteen years, Lucy rode horseback over the mountains from Sunderland to visit his grave. The children grew up and left home for various parts of the new nation.

A white neighbor then brought suit for some of the Prince property in Sunderland. Again Lucy Prince went to court. This time she entered Vermont's Supreme Court upon the advice of Isaac Ticknor, United States Senator, jurist, and later a governor of the state. Opposing the Prince claim was Royall Tyler, America's first playwright and novelist, and later a chief justice of the Vermont Supreme Court. After hearing all arguments, including those advanced by the sprightly black lady from Sunderland, the court ruled in favor of her claim.

It is reported that the judge leaned over to tell Lucy Prince that she had made a better argument than any he had heard from any Vermont attorney.

Lucy lived to be a vigorous ninety-one, active mentally and physically until her death in 1821. But she finally lost her Sunderland farm to the same destructive neighbor she had defeated at the governor's council. And in the year of her death the Massachusetts legislature established a committee to determine if the state should expel any black who entered.

The controversy over slavery had heightened. In so doing it weakened the foundation of black rights throughout the nation. An America heading toward conflict over slavery paid little heed to courageous black women such as Lucy Prince.

WILLIAM GOINGS

✦

GREENBURY LOGAN

Patriots of
the Lone Star Republic

Black people in the New World found that prejudice was greater among English-speaking people than among the Spanish, Portuguese, or French. One explanation has been the power of the Catholic Church in Latin America, and the ineffectiveness of the splintered Protestant churches in North America. This argument usually holds that in South America an all-powerful Church, believing in the immortal soul of the black, protected him from the worst abuses of the slave system.

In Latin America the Catholic Church encouraged attendance of blacks at services and sought conversions of slaves. To make its point, it asked owners to liberate slaves who became Christians and to allow them marriage in the Church. The Church promoted methods of emancipation, such as allowing slaves to purchase their liberty on the installment plan.

In the southern United States no churchman dared tell a slave master to free his slaves or even treat them humanely. The religious leaders were usually selected by slave owners and shaped their sermons to please them rather than a Christian conscience.

Above all, racial prejudice profoundly affected white relations with slaves and free blacks in North America. In Latin America this prejudice was present, but tempered by the Catholic Church's belief that each person, including a black, had a soul to be saved.

The history of early Texas, first under Spanish and Mexican rule, and then under the Lone Star Republic and finally under United States control, illustrates the changing attitudes toward blacks. In 1792 the Spanish conducted a census of their citizens living on the Texas plains. Of the 1,600 residents of the province almost 450 were black men and women. Apparently they had Spanish names and spoke Spanish. It is not known where they came from or how they became citizens of Spanish Texas. But the point is that they did, and were accepted as easily as other citizens were.

Before the arrival of the Americans, slavery had been outlawed in Texas. When Stephen and Moses Austin began bringing settlers from the United States to Texas, conflict with Mexico grew over this issue. Most Americans came from the South and were seeking land for planting, and meant to use slave labor. Since this was frontier land, and relatively easy escape to Mexico or neighboring Indian tribes was possible, perhaps only the most trusted slaves were brought along at first. There are many instances in early Texas history when black men and women stood by their masters during warfare with Indians. There are also many instances of desertion to nearby tribes, and some examples of blacks leading raids with Indians on white settlements. By 1834 Texas had twenty thousand American settlers and two thousand black slaves.

Free blacks came to Texas during its days as a Spanish and Mexican province. Perhaps the most remarkable one was William Goings (Goyans or Goyens), who lived in Nacagdoches as early as 1821. His blacksmith shop employed white laborers and black slaves. Within a decade he became a prominent and wealthy citizen, buying and selling Texas land at a handsome profit. He was married to a white woman from Georgia, and got along well with her brothers when they visited the couple's Texas home.

As a man who could read and write in English and Spanish and speak Cherokee and several other native languages, Goings became a trusted mediator between white and red people. "We believe him to be a man that will not tell a lie either for the White man or the Red man," Samuel Houston said of Goings. On several occasions he insisted that Goings negotiate for him with the Cherokees, and Houston visited his family as well.

When United States settlers rose against the Mexican government of Texas, men like Goings supported the Lone Star Republic. After the war the new government affirmed its protection for Goings and his lands. But he was the only black Texan who received this consideration.

Far more typical and much sadder was the experience of Greenbury Logan. In 1831 this free black answered the Austins' call to migrate to Texas. He personally met with Stephen Austin in Mexico and was granted land. "I love the country and did stay because I felt myself [more] a freeman than in the states," he later wrote.

In 1835 when Americans in Texas struck out for their own government, Logan joined them. Other free blacks also joined the revolutionaries. Early in the fighting Logan was severely wounded, and his injuries left him a cripple. He hobbled back to his land after the war to find a new situation confronting black Texas patriots like himself. American rule meant the supremacy of slavery and white domination. Rights of free blacks were canceled. This was how Logan described the turn of events to a member of the Texas Sixth Congress:

My discharge will show the man[n]er in which I discharged my duty as a free man and a sol[d]ier, but now look at my situation. Every previleg dear to a freeman is taken away and Logan is liable to be imposed upon by eny that chose to do it. No chance to collect a debt without [white] witnesses, no vote or say in eny way. Yet Logan is liable for Taxes as eny other person.

To his congressman Logan pointed out that he had sustained permanent injuries in the war that left him unable to work his land. "Everything that is deare to a freeman is taken from me," he wrote, and "I am too poor and embarrased and cannot leave honorable as I came." He had never asked for assistance before, and now only wanted his debts canceled. He said he would be willing to leave the land "though my blood has nearly all been shed for its rights."

There is no record of the fate of Greenbury Logan or his letter. The movement of Texas toward slavery, discrimination and Civil War is well known. Its black pioneers and patriots were forgotten as it turned to bloodshed over the right to hold slaves and gain new lands on which they would be held in bondage.

JOHN JONES

Prosperous Fighter
for Equal Rights

One of the few aspects of black history to escape the ne-
glect accorded the general subject was the underground
railroad. An account of this daring network of conductors and
homes that provided aid to fugitives managed to find its way
into history texts. However, the heroes and heroines were
usually pictured as white people motivated by religious convic-
tion to aid the poor slaves. Many whites did help largely because they deeply believed that bondage violated God's will.

But the real heroes of the underground railroad were the
blacks—those who had escaped slavery in a land where every
white face spelled danger, and those free blacks who risked all
to aid their brothers and sisters in flight. Blacks who helped
fugitives risked their own liberty. Since the laws did not recog-
nize their citizenship, they could be punished in ways whites
would never suffer. For aiding runaways, one free black was
sold as a slave himself.

Throughout the Old Northwest, blacks played a prominent part in the mysterious workings of the underground railroad. In Indiana the black leader was Reverend Chapman Harris, whose four sons aided him in the illegal and dangerous work of moving slaves across the Ohio River. Griffith Booth, another black Indianian who aided runaways, was once attacked by a Madison mob and another time thrown into the Ohio. Blacks were no less violent. Thirty black men almost beat an informer to death and then all refused to testify against their two accused ringleaders.

The Detroit station of the underground railroad became active in the 1830s. In 1833 antislavery black and white men attacked a sheriff, fracturing his skull and knocking out a few teeth. They were creating a diversion for a well-planned slave escape. Later this Detroit station was run by two determined blacks, William Lambert and George DeBaptiste. They called their organization "African-American Mysteries: The Order of the Men of Oppression."

To hide their work from the enemy, Lambert and DeBaptiste developed a complicated system of code words, signals, and hand grips. Fugitives were hidden near Lake Huron and provided with food, warmth, and new clothing. Before daybreak they were ferried to Cananda. "It was fight and run— danger at every turn," Lambert recalled years later, "but *that* we calculated upon, and were prepared for."

In Ohio the underground railroad ran one of the largest operations in the United States. So many fugitives crossed the Ohio River when it froze each year that Ohio was severely congested. The first book on this legendary undertaking was written by a black Ohio minister, Reverend William Mitchell. *The Underground Railroad from Slavery to Freedom*, published in England in 1860, told of Reverend Mitchell's activities as a "conductor" in Ross County from 1843 to 1855. Ohio had as many underground railroad agents as in all of the rest of the country, according to a scholarly account published in 1898. From 1830 to 1860 more than a thousand fugitives a year passed into Ohio and liberty.

In Chicago, Illinois, one of the leading figures in the underground railroad was a suave, prosperous black businessman. John Jones's aristocratic manner and personal wealth hid his illegal activities from his white neighbors. His personable ways even tended to make them forget that he and his wife, Mary, had arrived in 1845 with only $3.50 to their name.

Born to a German father and a free black mother in North Carolina, young Jones was apprenticed to a trader who promised to protect him from enslavement. It was not uncommon for blacks who were free, in the North or South, to be seized and forced into slavery. There was little protection from this crime, unless whites would vouch for the black person's safety. At the age of twenty-two, Jones secured his "free papers."

When John and Mary Jones arrived in Chicago, they were determined to make good. They set up a home, began to learn to read and write, and John Jones started a tailoring business. He pawned his watch to raise enough money to purchase a stove for his home and one for his store. A black grocer granted the family credit in the amount of $20. In time Jones massed a fortune of $100,000 and a reputation as a quiet, solid citizen.

But his real interest lay in aiding his people. Jones coordinated some of the underground railroad business with George DeBaptiste and worked hand in hand with other known and unknown figures, black and white, in its dangerous work.

One night Allan Pinkerton, later to head the U.S. Secret Service during the Civil War, brought the fiery John Brown to Jones's home. The three men planned the escape of eleven fugitives hidden in Chicago. Brown and Jones had met before, but this would be the last meeting, for Brown was headed for Harpers Ferry and martyrdom.

As the nation moved toward war over slavery, Jones's home

UNITED STATES OF AMERICA,

STATE OF ILLINOIS, } ss. { To all to whom these Presents may come—GREETING:
Madison County,

𝕶𝖓𝖔𝖜 𝖄𝖊, That *John Tony* a person of Color, about _twenty seven_ year of age, _post five_ feet _six_ inches high, _Mulatto_ complexion,

has exhibited, presented and filed, in the Office of the Clerk of the Circuit Court of the County and State aforesaid, a **CERTIFICATE,** duly authenticated, of **FREEDOM,** as such person of Color *has a scarr over the left Eye Brow a scratch across the cheek bone a scarr on the left shin bone Taylor to Trade*

Now, therefore, I, **WM. TYLER BROWN,** Clerk of the Circuit Court of Madison County, State of Illinois, **CERTIFY,** That said *John Tony* is a FREE PERSON OF COLOR, a resident or citizen of the State of Illinois, and entitled to be respected accordingly, in Person and Property, at all times and places, in the due prosecution of _his_ Lawful concerns.

In Testimony whereof, I have, to these Presents, signed my name, and affixed the Seal of said Court, at Edwardsville, this 2 8th day of *November* in the year of our Lord one thousand eight hundred and forty-four

Wm. T. Brown Clerk.

The freedom papers given to John Jones. (CHICAGO HISTORICAL SOCIETY)

in Chicago became a headquarters for black and white abolitionists. When Frederick Douglass and other prominent figures came to town, they usually enjoyed the hospitality of John and Mary Jones. Increasingly, Jones joined the agitation against slavery as a speaker and organizer. When the Illinois legislature passed a law in 1853 forbidding blacks to enter the state, he led the opposition. He lectured throughout the state on the rights of blacks, contributed money to the campaign, and encouraged other blacks to enter the fight for equality.

Despite his escalating part in the struggle for black rights, Jones expanded his business during the 1850s and purchased a large store at 119 Dearborn Street. He was able to find time to help blacks in his state organize conventions to protest discrimination. He became a well-known black spokesman as the nation entered the Civil War.

In 1864 he wrote a pamphlet denouncing the "black laws" that restricted the rights of his people in Illinois. *The Black Laws of Illinois and a Few Reasons Why They Should Be Repealed* struck at the vast array of northern laws that kept black men from serving on juries, from bringing suits against whites in courts, voting in elections, or attending schools, and using hospitals and other public facilities with whites. As a businessman, Jones addressed part of his argument to the white business community. If their black wagon drivers were robbed, he told them, they could not testify against the white criminals in any court in Illinois.

One of the points made by the author was that he paid taxes on $30,000 in property but could not vote. In less than a year petitions were pouring into the Illinois legislature demanding repeal of the black laws, and in January 1865 they were revoked.

The end of the Civil War a few months later did not mean the end of black struggle. President Andrew Johnson sat in the White House, and he had little use for black voting rights in the

South. He believed in leaving the ex-slaves of the South to the tender care of their former masters. Frederick Douglass, John Jones, and a black delegation visited President Johnson at the White House. They implored him to provide a basic protection to blacks by arming them with the vote. The President curtly dismissed them, saying their demands were provoking a "race war."

By then a prosperous and noted Illinois citizen, John Jones had twice won election to the Cook County (Chicago) Board of Commissioners. He used his position to oppose the segregated school system. During the later years of his life, he donated money to many charities. He died in 1879 and was mourned by white and black Chicagoans. He had "made it"—but without giving up his principles or forgetting his color. He had used his wealth to help his people and his country.

EDMONIA LEWIS

From Chippewa Nation
to Famed Sculptor

Born in Greenhigh, Ohio, to a Chippewa mother and a free black father, Edmonia Lewis was destined to become America's first successful black sculptor. Though her exciting life took her to sophisticated Boston and Rome, she often longed to return to the simple tribal life she remembered as a young girl.

Her mother had been born in Albany, where she made and sold moccasins. After her marriage, she and her husband took up life in white civilization. However, she often left their home to live with her own people, taking her daughter and son with her. "Until I was twelve years old," Edmonia later recalled, "I led this wandering life, fishing and swimming." Like her mother, she also made moccasins.

When her mother was dying, she sent for her daughter and made her promise to live three years with the Chippewas. This

Edmonia did, making baskets and embroidering moccasins, and taking them into town to sell. Her early schooling was largely a failure, for teachers found her "too wild—they could do nothing with me."

But her brother, who had traveled to California to dig for gold, returned in 1856 and persuaded Edmonia to attend Oberlin College. In 1833 this new college opened its doors for the first time to women, including black women. The college and town nearby attracted anti-slavery people and many blacks. It became a leading station for the famous underground railroad. Five different routes converged on the town. One slave catcher complained Oberlin was an "old buzzard's nest where the Negroes who arrive over the underground railroad are regarded as dear children." The students at Oberlin took an active part aiding runaways. This caused the Ohio legislature to try four times to revoke the college charter.

At Oberlin, Edmonia Lewis studied Latin and Greek and became interested in sculpture (though no course was given in it). Then, in her fourth year, and after enjoying Oberlin, a tragedy brought her college career to a close. Two of her white friends were found poisoned, and Edmonia was charged with their murder. Her trial lasted several weeks and ended with her acquittal. Though carried joyfully from court on the shoulders of her fellow students, she felt discouraged. She "thought of returning to the wild life again; but my love of sculpture forbade it."

She left for Boston, where she met prominent abolitionists and was introduced to a leading Boston sculptor. Within a year she was producing medallions and busts that were considered excellent. Her first important work to attract attention was a bust of Colonel Robert Shaw, the white commander of the 54th Massachusetts Regiment, the first black northern regiment in the Civil War.

During the Civil War Edmonia supported herself by her

Edmonia Lewis achieved fame with her sculpting and painting.

sculpture, laboring long hours and working quickly to produce enough to live on. Some felt she worked too fast and told her this. Others praised her enthusiastically. She told abolitionist writer Lydia Maria Child, one of her severest critics, "I don't want you to go to praise me, for I know praise is not good for me. Some praise me because I am a colored girl, and I don't want that kind of praise. I had rather you would point out my defects, for that will teach me something."

In 1865 Edmonia Lewis left for Rome to study sculpture at the studio of a famous Italian master. She made friends as easily as she had done at Oberlin, though some remarked negatively about her "masculine look," careless clothes, and "personal peculiarities." She also painted, and her works were purchased by Benjamin Disraeli and other noted Europeans.

Back in Boston, she did an admired bust of Henry Wadsworth Longfellow. Before he agreed to sit for her, she secretly made a likeness of him by waiting at a street corner he passed each day. His image in mind, she hurried back to her studio and worked on her clay. Her busts of Longfellow, Abraham Lincoln, and Senator Charles Sumner established her as the first important black sculptor. Her fame in Europe was greater than in the United States, but she enjoyed success on both sides of the Atlantic.

One of her most interesting pieces, "The Freedwoman on First Hearing of Her Liberty," shows a freed black woman on her knees praying to God for her redemption. A broken chain attached to a huge ball lies before her. In remarking on this figure, Edmonia Lewis said, "Yes, so was my race treated in the market and elsewhere. It tells with much eloquence a painful story." Her remarks were not meant to be immodest, but rather to demonstrate the point of her work.

Today her sculptures are rare sought-after collectors' items. Though her work was interesting and admirable, it is more appreciated as a first artistic effort than as a lasting, memorable contribution.

DRED SCOTT

The Slave Whose Case
Moved a Nation

For a century after the Supreme Court denied him his freedom, the black man known to most American students was the slave Dred Scott. Actually, textbooks have told little about Scott except that his master had taken him into free states and territories of the Northwest. On this basis the slave had filed for his freedom. But the high court ruled against him in a landmark decision that paved the way to the Civil War.

Though he has appeared in every history text and social studies course, Dred Scott has remained invisible as a person. His life, wishes, and even his family have been overshadowed by the court decision that bears his name. Dred Scott emerges from history books as a figure without normal roots or feelings; yet he was married and had two children. When he took his case to court, it was to win their liberty as well. Scott is also pictured as an ignorant person whose own case mystified him, and who had little interest in its outcome. This ignores several facts, particularly his ten-year court fight for the freedom of his family.

Born in the late eighteenth century, Scott was raised in St. Louis. Although he was married, his wife and two male children were sold away from him. There is no record of how he felt, for no one cared to ask slaves about the sale of their families. In 1834 Scott was taken by his master, a U.S. Army surgeon, from St. Louis to Illinois and to Fort Snelling in the Wisconsin Territory. There he again married. His new wife was Harriet, another slave. They had two children, Eliza and Lizzie.

Several books, including the *Dictionary of American Biography*, state that Dred Scott was "shiftless and unreliable, and therefore frequently unemployed and without means to support his family." Only a master would have assumed that a slave was shiftless. Slaves viewed a negative response to forced labor as normal and intelligent. Why be anything but shiftless when one's labors were only to benefit another? A slave could only be "unemployed" if his master wished him to be. Also, according to slavery's code, the master, not the husband-slave, had the responsibility to "support his family."

Dred Scott was hardly a stupid, shiftless, or uninformed man. When his family's freedom was concerned, he was courageous, persistent, and hard-working. Once, while living in St. Louis, he had fled his master to hide briefly in the Lucas swamps, a haven for slave runaways. After a long stay in the West, Scott, a family man with a wife and two children to think about, shifted tactics to gain freedom.

First he approached his master's wife and offered to purchase his family's freedom. She turned down the offer. Next Scott took the $300 he had been saving, hired a lawyer, and brought suit for his family's liberty before Judge Krum in St. Louis. These are hardly the actions of a "shiftless" man, or one who cared or knew little about liberty. Possibly the $300 Scott had

Dred Scott and his wife, Harriet.

saved came from extra work undertaken to raise money for this purpose.

For ten years and ten months the Dred Scott case dragged on in the United States courts. The old slave maintained that since his family had lived on free United States territory, it was entitled to freedom. During this time Scott received some financial aid to carry on his legal battle. Anti-slavery forces helped because they thought a decision in Scott's favor would aid their cause. Scott was willing to cooperate with them since he needed their financial aid, and did not oppose their aims.

Finally, the U.S. Supreme Court ruled against the Scotts.

Indeed, this decision virtually opened all lands in the West to
slavery and precipitated a major crisis over slavery's growth.
Abraham Lincoln and the new Republican party made the most
of the case, saying the only way to halt slavery's extension to
the West was to vote Republican. Anti-slavery forces grew and,
within three years, helped elect Lincoln President of the United
States.

By the time the court ruled against them, the Scotts had a
new master who was willing to liberate them. Soon they were
free and at work in St. Louis. Harriet Scott ran a laundry business. Dred Scott—"shiftless Dred Scott"—worked in a hotel
and also helped his wife with her laundry business.

However, years of slave life and declining health had taken a
toll. A year after achieving his freedom Dred Scott died; the
next year Harriet Scott died.

Throughout his life Dred Scott battled as best he could for
liberty. He aimed not to precipitate a crisis over slavery or win
a place in history but to free his family from bondage. In the
end he was successful.

Despite overwhelming odds, repeated failures, the onset of
old age, and rapidly deteriorating health, Dred Scott per-
severed until victory. School texts have called persons who
have done far less "heroic."

The family of Dred Scott is long dead and the Supreme
Court decision remembered only as a tragic chapter in our history. But the distortions about Scott remain. Some of our leading historians have failed to see the Scotts through the eyes of
black people. They have insisted on viewing this black family
through the eyes of a slaveholder class that has been dead for
more than a century. That is inexcusable.

The picture of Dred Scott as too stupid and too lazy to fight
for his own freedom is wrong. It not only distorts the truth,
but it keeps us from understanding his determination to be free
and equal.

GEORGE WASHINGTON

Founder of Centralia,
Washington

In the years before the Civil War a man named George Washington was forced to leave Illinois because he could not post a bond to guarantee his good behavior in the state. George Washington was black and the posting of a bond was only one of many laws restricting blacks from the full enjoyment of their rights. In this respect the western states and territories before the Civil War were no better than the eastern ones, and sometimes a little worse.

In western states the leading issue at their constitutional conventions had nothing to do with government, rights, or taxes. The issue was whether to admit blacks or how to restrict them. The black George Washingtons of America had to expend more energy, possess more courage, and endure more man-made hardships than other pioneers.

It mattered not one bit whether white westerners favored or hated slavery; they all opposed blacks settling in their lands.

Horace Greeley, the famous editor who urged Americans to "go west, young man," made clear the new lands "shall be reserved for the benefit of the white Caucasian race." Facing the question of black migration to Indiana, a delegate to the state's 1850 constitutional convention simply said, "It would be better to kill them off at once, if there is no other way to get rid of them."

The law that drove George Washington from Illinois was only one of many against blacks in the West. Indiana enacted the first, a law in 1803 prohibiting a black to testify at any trial involving whites. A few years later it forbade blacks from voting, and some years later it placed a special tax of three dollars a year on all blacks. Ohio law required blacks to submit a $500 bond to insure their good behavior in the state. This law was not enforced. However, in 1829 when whites in Cincinnati felt they faced too much black labor competition, they demanded its enforcement. Even before the law could be invoked, a white mob surged through the black community, looting, burning homes, and driving the residents before them.

By the 1840s the white hand of discrimination stretched from the Atlantic coast inland to the expanding western territories. Abolitionist Gerrit Smith of New York described conditions in states of the Old Northwest as well as his own when he said:

Even the noblest black is denied that which is free to the vilest white. The omnibus, the car, the ballot-box, the jury box, the halls of legislation, the army, the public lands, the school, the church, the lecture room, the social circle, the table, are all either absolutely or virtually denied to him.

In light of these conditions, the career and attitudes of George Washington form a remarkable chapter in American history.

Born in Virginia as was his more famous namesake, George Washington had a white mother and a slave father. For reasons that are not known, his mother gave him in adoption to a white couple heading westward. After a brief stay in Ohio, the Washington family moved to Missouri. Without formal schooling young George learned reading, writing, and arithmetic.

He needed far more than this for survival on the frontier. He became an expert marksman with rifle or revolver, and picked up skills as a miller, distiller, tanner, cook, weaver, and spinner. Operating a sawmill in St. Joseph, he found that his abilities mattered little when a white man was determined to cheat a black man. One customer refused to pay him for a load of lumber. When Washington tried to sue him in court, his case was thrown out because he was black and had no rights to sue.

George Washington became well-known in Missouri for his skills and strength. Over six feet tall and almost two hundred pounds, he was respected as a muscular youth determined to succeed.

Missouri was not the place for him, and so he moved on to Illinois. When the state demanded a bond he could not afford, he continued into the West. With his foster parents, Washington left in a wagon train from Iowa in 1850. It took four months to reach the Oregon Territory. There the Washingtons built a crude home and their son took a lumberjack job.

In his thirties now and doing nicely, Washington staked out a claim on a 640-acre plot. Because Oregon law banned settlement to blacks, his father placed the land in his own name. Washington grew cereal and vegetable crops, and together with his father raised cattle and operated an inn and ferry. When the Oregon law was changed, the land was put in the name of George Washington. His land was located at the junction of two rivers, the exact point where Centralia, Washington, would later stand.

In the years after the Civil War his good fortune continued. He was able to repay his parents for the land they had purchased for him. After their death he married an attractive black

George Washington was born in Virginia, as was his more famous namesake. (OREGON HISTORICAL SOCIETY)

widow named Mary Jane. Together they prospered. In 1872, when the Northern Pacific Railroad was built across his land, he established a town called Centerville, halfway between the Columbia River and Puget Sound. It eventually became Centralia.

To aid the town, Washington sold lots for $5 to anyone who would agree to build on the land they purchased. This prevented the land from falling into the hands of speculators who only bought it to resell at a higher rate. To buy a plot from

George Washington, a man had to agree to build a house worth at least a hundred dollars. With some of his profits Washington donated land for parks, a cemetery, and churches. He also achieved a reputation for aiding the town's less fortunate settlers.

When his first wife died, the founder of Centralia remarried. In his mid-seventies he had a son with his second wife.

The panic of 1893 brought hard times to almost every door in Centralia. Residents had little food and less money to pay their mortgages. George Washington became a one-man relief agency. His wagons brought rice, flour, sugar, meat, and lard from as far away as Portland. He loaned funds to people in debt to banks and creditors. Whenever he could, he hired local people to work for him. During this crisis, a recent authority on Centralia has written, "he saved the town."

At eighty-eight Washington went out for a buggy ride and was thrown into the road. In August 1905 he died as a result of the injuries. Centralia citizens gave their black friend the biggest funeral in the town's history. The mayor proclaimed a day of mourning. Washington's body was carried to a church he had donated, on land he had donated, and then buried in a cemetery he had donated—entirely fitting for the founder of the town.

The city's park still bears the name of this dedicated man. He had braved the dangers of the frontier and the hatred of men to make his striking contribution to the West. Many who knew him personally, and many who never did, benefited from his skills, resourceful mind, and compassionate heart.

GEORGE WASHINGTON BUSH

Cutting Color Lines
in the Far West

In 1844 presidential candidate James A. Polk was steaming mad about the British occupation of the Oregon Territory. His slogan became "54° 40' or Fight," referring to the line the United States wished to draw demarcating for itself the entire Oregon Territory and ousting the British permanently from it. In a close election, Polk's forces carried the day.

The Oregon Territory question was settled without a shot being fired. Although the United States did not gain all the land it desired, it did receive a very large portion of this territory. The successful claim of the United States was based on a settlement in the Puget Sound region by an Irish immigrant, Michael Simmons, and his black companion, George Washington Bush. These men were very different but both had good reasons for settling there. Simmons, who as an Irishman had no love for the British, resented British officials telling him to keep clear of their Columbia River valley. He had no interest in protecting their lucrative fur business in the Puget Sound region if it meant he could not settle where he chose.

Simmons's friend, George Bush, had a different problem. The government had prohibited blacks from settling on the part of the Oregon Territory already controlled by the Americans. To avoid this law Simmons, Bush and his party pushed northward into the British-claimed part of Oregon. It is ironic that Bush's escape from America's discrimination led to the successful United States claim to the land where he did finally settle. It is even more ironic that American control of this new northerly land again brought Bush under the "black laws" passed by the Oregon legislature. It took Michael Simmons, once he was elected to the Oregon legislature, to exempt this black pioneer from the laws.

George Bush was a daring if quiet man, and one not easily discouraged. His early life is hard to piece together. Some authorities say he fought at the Battle of New Orleans with Andrew Jackson. Others say he was a Quaker and was opposed to violence. Some reports say he came from Missouri where he owned many cattle and had been a successful rancher. It is certain that in 1844 Bush, his white wife, and five children were part of a wagon train heading west from Missouri.

John Minto, a pioneer, met Bush and his family during this trip. Bush was very concerned about how his family would be treated anywhere in America. Minto also discovered that Bush was aiding two other families in the caravan. This may well account for the group's solidarity in pledging themselves to protect Bush against discrimination. Bush seems to have played a leading role in the expedition. His advice, recalled by another traveler, was short and to the point: "Boys, you are going through a hard country. You have guns and ammunition. Take my advice: anything you see as big as a blackbird, kill and eat it."

The party led by Simmons and Bush pushed into the British-held part of Oregon and found jobs in forestry. Soon the Bush family gained a reputation for aiding newcomwers to the area. A few miles south of a place called Tumwater laid out by Simmons, the Bush family settled on what today is called Bush Prairie.

During the winter of 1852 Bush's generosity was put to a severe test. The grain supply on Puget Sound was low, and speculators were paying high prices for the wheat crop. Farmers began selling their crops without regard to their neighbors' future needs. When speculators rode out to Bush Prairie and offered Bush a high price for his wheat, he turned them down. "I'll keep my grain." he told them. "so that my neighbors will have enough to live on and for seeding their fields in the spring. They have no money to pay your fancy prices, and I don't intend to see them want for anything I can provide them with."

Until his death in 1863, George Bush maintained good relations with all he met in the Far West—white, red, and black men and women. He was considered an amiable and friendly man.

It was all the more remarkable that Bush had succeeded in a state with some of the most obnoxious black laws in the Union. Oregon's territorial legislature once passed a law expelling all black males in two years. Black females were given an extra year to leave. For all who ignored the expulsion a whipping every six months was designated. This law was later altered—those who stayed were obligated to labor without pay for a certain amount of time. In 1859 when Oregon entered the Union, it became the first free state to be admitted by Congress with a black exclusion clause.

After the death of their father, the Bush sons carried on in his tradition of farming skill and public service. One son raised a prize wheat crop that was later placed on exhibit at the

Smithsonian Institution in Washington, D.C. In 1889 William Owen Bush was elected to the Washington State House, where he served two terms. By their effort and example, the Bush family showed the potential blacks would realize when given the opportunity.

William Owen Bush, son of pioneer settler George Washington Bush, at the time of his election to the Washington State House of Representatives.

WILLIAM LEIDESDORFF

Public-Minded
San Franciscan

In 1841, when William Leidesdorff sailed a 160-ton schooner into San Francisco Bay, California had already become a community of many racial and ethnic groups. The son of a Danish planter and an African mother from the Virgin Islands, Leidesdorff must have felt quite at home. He probably needed such acceptance, for his voyage to the American continent grew out of an unsuccessful love affair.

At this time California was an outlying Mexican province. By 1790 18 percent of the residents of San Francisco, 24 percent of San José, 20 percent of Santa Barbara, and 18 percent of Monterey were of African descent. Los Angeles was founded by 44 persons comprising eleven families. Of these 26 were black, 2 were Caucasians, and the others were Indians or of mixed Indian-Caucasian ancestry.

Neither the Catholic Church nor Spanish authorities ever

sought to set people apart by their skin color or their ancestors, although Spanish blood was considered superior. When couples arrived at the decision to marry, the Church and civil authorities did not stand in their way. Blacks, Caucasians, Indians, and foreigners (from Europe or South America) were free to marry whom they chose.

A darker skin color did not keep a Californian from attaining wealth or political power. Maria Rita Valdez was the grand-daughter of two of the black founding members of Los Angeles. She owned Rancho Rodeo de Las Aguas, better known today as Beverly Hills. Francisco Reyes, another black resident of the province, owned the San Fernando Valley. In the 1790s he sold it and became mayor of Los Angeles. By 1845 Pio Pico was governor of California. In the 1790 census his grandmother had been listed as a "mulata," meaning a mixture of black and white parents.

When Leidesdorff arrived in San Francisco, the town had little to recomend it other than its lovely views. William Tecumseh Sherman recalled: "At that time there was not a shod horse in California, not a tavern, hotel, or even a common wagon road." Leidesdorff did much to change that—to put the city on the road to progress, comfort, and education.

In a short time Leidesdorff, who did not arrive poor, became very wealthy. He owned a 35,000-acre estate he called Rio del Rancho Americana. From the outset he cultivated an interest in the American minority in this Mexican land and identified strongly with United States aims. In 1845 he became a United States subconsul and worked closely with those vitally interested in bringing California into the Union. This probably made Leidesdorff the first black diplomat in United States history.

As a prosperous and popular San Franciscan, Leidesdorff made several unusual contributions to the development of the region. He introduced the first steamboat to San Francisco Bay,

William Leidesdorff. (CALIFORNIA STATE LIBRARY)

and this naturally caused a stir. He also organized the city's first horse race, and racing became a popular form of entertainment and gambling. In 1846 he opened the city's first hotel, the City Hotel, which became a meeting place for important San Franciscans.

Young residents of the city and their mothers knew Leidesdorff as the man who helped establish the first public school, a one-room shack where pupils could learn their reading, writing, and arithmetic. By this time the young innovator was treasurer for the San Francisco City Council.

When American troops landed in California and read a proclamation in Spanish to the local population, it was Leidesdorff who had spent the night before translating it. Not only did he help establish the new American government in power, but offered his huge home for a fancy-dress ball for the leading United States officers. By this time he owned large tracts of land in San Francisco and near a place called Sutter's Mill, where gold was first discovered.

Suddenly in 1848 Leidesdorff was struck down by what people then called brain fever, but which now is called typhus. He was still a young man when he died, at age forty-one. His great real estate holdings, estimated at more than a million dollars, were bought up by people who found San Francisco more attractive because of his efforts.

The prospectors who stayed at the City Hotel, the children who sat in the first public school, the men who enjoyed the horse races he started, and those who proudly baosted that San Francisco had a steamboat before the Gold Rush—these were some of the beneficiaries of Leidesdorff's ingenuity, generosity, and public-mindedness.

View of San Francisco in 1847. Buildings and land owned by Leidesdorff are at the lower left of the bay.

ROBERT T. HICKMAN

Fleeing West
to Freedom

One of the slaveholders' enduring fantasies had been the picture of their bondsmen laboring contentedly in the southern sun. Because they wished to convince themselves and the world that their slaves were not exploited or mistreated, they created the myth of the happy black. Each year hundreds upon hundreds of slaves refuted this notion by fleeing their masters, striking out in every direction for freedom.

Traveling by night and hiding by day, they headed north to the free states or south to Mexico or Florida or west to the free territories. Sometimes with the aid of the underground railroad, but usually only by themselves and without any organized help, they left. Reward notices printed in southern papers revealed that those who escaped had probably left to join relatives sold away from them by slave masters.

Ex-slaves who had escaped to Canada or elsewhere returned south to help relatives find their way to liberty. In so doing they risked their own safety, and perhaps their lives. Slave-holders sought to crush this movement by brutality and death, and by offering rewards for the recovery of those who escaped. No matter how hard they tried, however, those who owned men, women, and children could not end the black thirst for liberty.

Even in the 1850s, after Congress passed a strict Fugitive Slave Law that severely punished aiding slave escapees, the drive for freedom only increased. A convention of fugitive slaves from Canada met that year in New York State to pledge its unflagging aid to those still in chains. The participants' depiction of slavery, underlined by their own daring escapes, destroyed any myth of black acceptance of the institution:

So galling was our bondage, that to escape from it, we suffered the loss of all things, and braved every peril, and endured every hardship. Some of us left parents, some wives, some children. Some of us were wounded with guns and dogs, as we fled. Some of us secreted ourselves in the suffocating holds of ships. Nothing was so dreadful to us as slavery.

Slaves who set out for the North had only the North Star to guide them. Masters had made sure that their slaves knew little of the outside world, and less of geography or of the free North and Canada. To prevent flight, slaves were told that Yankees were cannibals who might eat them, and abolitionists who aided them were really planning to resell them in the West Indies. Laws prevented slaves from learning how to read and write, and some masters kept them from learning how to swim.

Yet flight from bondage marked the entire era of slavery in America. Into an unknown, uncharted, and unfriendly world black men, women, and children set out to search for a haven. They left their plantations knowing that the punishment for escape was severe—branding, beating, being sold further south, or worse.

Some slave escapes showed remarkable valor and daring.

Harriet Tubman, who escaped from bondage herself, returned nineteen times during the 1850s to help some three hundred others make their way to liberty. A price of $50,000 was placed on her head, but she was never caught. At times entire groups of blacks made their way northward together, led by nothing more than their wish for liberty.

Robert T. Hickman, born a slave in Missouri in 1831, led a dramatic mass escape to Minnesota during the Civil War. Although he labored as a rail-splitter, Hickman was allowed to learn to read and write. He was even permitted to preach to his fellow slaves, but under the careful eyes of whites on the plantation where he lived.

The Civil War stimulated the black drive for liberty. As slaves learned that Yankees were fighting their masters on the battlefield, their own interest in the war increased. News of battles was transmitted from one slave to another, from one plantation to another. This "grapevine telegraph" kept slaves informed about the latest developments and their own chances for liberty. Slaveholders increased their patrols during the war but it did little good, for slaves were on the move. Many made it to the Union lines in wagons or on foot. Long before emancipation became a policy of the Lincoln administration, slaves decided to join the Yankees.

In Boone County, Missouri, Hickman and a large group of blacks agreed to make a break for the northern states. Together they built a large raft. Then, one night they gathered at the raft and sailed northward up the Mississippi. Estimates of the number in the group have ranged up to two hundred.

It is unclear whether or not the group made their way to St. Paul without help. Some stories have it that Union soldiers aided them or that their raft was towed northward behind a steamer. The group called themselves "pilgrims."

Those who remained in St. Paul formed the Pilgrim Baptist Church with Hickman as their minister. He was formally ordained in 1877. But others spread to outlaying sections of the West. Still others joined the Union army, which by then was accepting black enlistees. By the time the war ended, more than 200,000 black men had served in the Union army or navy.

Robert Hickman led slaves to freedom in Minnesota. (MINNESOTA HISTORICAL SOCIETY)

MARY FIELDS

"Stagecoach Mary"

When tall, powerfully built, fifty-two-year-old Mary Fields arrived in Cascade in the Montana Territory in 1884, there were few other blacks. The state of Montana was still to be realized five years in the future, and the sprawling prairie had about 191 black men and 155 black women. Neighbors may have wondered if the newcomer with the broad shoulders was typical of the new settlers.

Born in a Tennessee log cabin during the administration of President Andrew Jackson (also from Tennessee), Mary Fields and the President had some common traits. They were both ambitious, daring, and liked a good fight. But in Montana life started peacefully for Mary Fields.

With Mother Amadeus, an Ursuline nun, she arrived ready to work at St. Peter's Catholic Mission near Cascade. Mother Amadeus came to start a school for Indian women, and Mary

Fields came along to help. The two women spent eight severe winters before the school was built. In freezing temperature they huddled over a fire in their log cabin.

Mary Fields did much of the heavy work around the place. She hauled lumber, drove a wagon, and picked up supplies from town. Perhaps because of the cold, she took to wearing two sets of clothing. Over a man's pair of pants she wore a long dress, an apron, and then a man's overcoat. This covering for her two-hundred-pound frame made her a notable sight in Montana.

Excitement soon entered her life at the Catholic mission. One night while hauling freight to St. Peter's, wolves attacked her wagon. The horses bolted. Wagon, supplies, and a surprised Mary Fields landed on the Montana prairie. It was a lonely and fearful night. With a rifle and pistol, and an iron determination not to fall asleep, Mary Fields kept the wolves at bay.

Another time during a bitter winter, she was driving her wagon from Cascade to the mission. A light snowfall turned to a blizzard whipped by strong winds. It was no use going forward, for it was not possible to see ahead more than a few feet. Mary Fields got down from the wagon and waited out the storm, walking back and forth all night to keep from freezing.

The nuns liked Mary Fields despite her pugnacious manner. They put up with the fact that she insisted on carrying guns and having fights with the hired hands. But one day she went too far. A dispute with a handyman led to gunfire as the two shot it out. No one was injured or killed, but everyone was shaken up. The bishop in Helena ordered Mother Amadeus to send Mary Fields away. Gunplay on consecrated ground was unacceptable.

But Mother Amadeus only sent her friend as far as Cascade and there helped her begin a restaurant. It failed. Some say Mary Fields was too good-hearted, feeding alike those who could pay, those who promised to pay, and those who could

*Mary Fields, known
as Stagecoach Mary.*

not pay at all. Again Mother Amadeus helped her establish the
business and again it failed. Perhaps inside work did not agree
with Mary Fields.

In 1895 a mail route was established between Cascade and
the Catholic Mission. Mother Amadeus helped Mary Fields
land the job of carrying the mail. In her sixties, she delivered
mail in clear weather and storms for eight years.

Later she took a job driving a stagecoach. From then on she was known as "Stagecoach Mary."

In her seventies she settled down to a laundry business. Mother Amadeus had been ordered to a mission in Alaska, and Stagecoach Mary was too old to accompany her. But she had many friends now in Cascade. The New Cascade hotel gave her free meals, and townsfolk helped pay for and rebuild her house when it burned to the ground.

But not everyone knew her or her reputation. One man walked into her laundry, picked up his clean clothes, and walked out without paying his bill. What could a woman do about it, he must have thought. He soon found out. She trotted after him, tapped him on the shoulder, and waited for him to turn around. As he faced her, she landed her heavy fist on his jaw and he went sprawling on the sidewalk. She walked back, announcing, "His bill's been paid in full." Not bad for a seventy-year-old woman.

During her years in town she took to smoking cigars and drinking in saloons with the men. No one questioned this, and some insist the town passed a law allowing her to drink in saloons.

Did she ever mellow? Some Cascadians thought so. They tell how Mary Fields took baby-sitting jobs. She gave schoolchildren candy on her birthday. Some say the schools closed that day so everyone could enjoy the birthday surprises of tough old Mary Fields.

A simple wooden cross marks the grave of this gun-toting female pioneer in Cascade's Hillside Cemetery.

RUSHING FOR GOLD

BIDDY MASON

Fighting for Freedom
in California

On January 24, 1848, gold was discovered in California. John A. Sutter, a Swiss immigrant who owned the land on the south fork of the American River, and his partner, James W. Marshall, made the discovery with a gang of Indian laborers. They all agreed to keep the bright yellow metal pieces that they had found a secret. They did not succeed.

By the end of the year California's population had doubled. Then the President of the United States announced the find, and within another year the population had soared to ten times its original size. In 1852, when California had been a state in the Union for only two years, its population reached almost a quarter of a million people. Of these, a hundred thousand considered themselves prospectors.

Who were these newcomers and where did they come from? Some were the Indians, Spaniards, or Mexicans who had always lived there. Another entire group were the Chinese, who came across the Pacific to make their fortune. Many crossed the plains in covered wagons. Others sailed from the eastern seaboard to Panama, crossed overland, and then continued their journey by ship to San Francisco. Still others sailed around Cape Horn to reach their destination.

Biddy Mason walked. She trudged behind the three hundred wagons of her master's caravan from Mississippi to California. This thirty-two-year-old slave had the job of keeping the cattle together during the long voyage across the continent, so she had to walk.

Biddy Mason was one of untold numbers of slaves brought by southern owners to labor in the gold fields. White miners, who resented the presence of any competition in the fields, immediately took action to halt the use of nonwhite labor in the mines. A "foreign miners' tax" was imposed on Indians, Spaniards, Mexicans, blacks, and Chinese. Its aim was not to raise revenue but to keep nonwhites away from the mines. Periodically white miners concluded the tax was not working efficiently. They took matters into their own hands and drove out nonwhites with threats and violence. In 1850 when a Texas slaveholding family arrived with fifteen blacks at Rose's Bar, whites called a protest meeting that resolved: "No slave or Negro should own claims or even work in the mines." A second meeting informed the Texans to remove their slaves or they would be forcibly removed. The Texans apparently left.

White resentment of black miners stemmed from a widely held belief that blacks had a mysterious power to detect gold. This was clearly unfair competition. Every effort was made to keep blacks from using their special power in the California gold fields.

Throughout the 1850s, however, slaveholders brought their human property to the new state. Many blacks managed to labor in the gold fields despite the opposition of whites. Alvin

Biddy Mason walked from Mississippi to California.

Coffey, brought to the mines by his Missouri master, earned five thousand dollars in a short time. Although his master had agreed to let Coffey purchase the freedom of his family, instead he merely seized his money and sold him. Coffey went on to convince his new owner to let him work the gold fields to raise money for his family's liberty. This time he was successful, and by 1860 the Coffeys were free and prosperous residents of Tehama County.

There must have been something in the air of Gold Rush California that stimulated thoughts of freedom. Many slaves made the effort, and some succeeded. Biddy Mason, hearing that her master planned to return to Mississippi, decided the

time had come to liberate herself and her three daughters. With
the aid of the local sheriff, she and her daughters won their
freedom. They remained to settle down in California.

Mrs. Mason and her daughters were only a few of many who
fought for liberty. On the streets of San José, San Francisco,
and Sacramento black men and women battled with their white
masters. Many of these cases ended up in courts, and sometimes blacks found white lawyers ready to defend them. Judges
also aided at times, by bending interpretations of California
laws. One judge freed a black man who admitted he was owned
by the Missouri man who claimed him. Sorry, said the judge,
since a black man's testimony could not be taken by a court,
this admission was not acceptable. The black man went free
and the bewildered slaveholder returned to Missouri minus one
smiling slave.

Free blacks played an important part in the escape of many
slaves. Mary Ellen Pleasant, who divided her time between
running a brothel and aiding her race, rode into rural sections
of the state to rescue people held in bondage. The entire black
community of San Francisco received a warning from one judge
for the "insolent and defiant" and "dangerous" way they inter-
fered with those who were arresting slaves. At Stockton a free
black who was seized as a slave and whose freedom papers were
destroyed was subsequently liberated by a mob.

Biddy Mason and her family were among the lucky ones.
They began their free life in California by working hard and
saving carefully. Through investments, Mrs. Mason purchased
large amounts of real estate. Soon she had land to donate for
schools, churches, and hospitals. Her generosity also took a
more personal form. She aided flood victims and brought food
to men in the state's jails. A person who had walked to California from Mississippi as a slave knew what it meant to be oppressed and friendless. By the time she died in 1891, Mrs.
Mason had won many friends of both races.

MIFFLIN W. GIBBS

Active Crusader
for Black Equality

Like a huge magnet, California drew the adventurous, the ambitious, and the treacherous to its Golden Gate. Indians, Chinese, Chileans, Mexicans, Europeans, New Englanders, and southerners—in short, people of all races and nationalities—flocked to seek their fortune.

They came seeking instant wealth, but few found it. Excitement turned to pain, and hunger mounted. Those who struck it rich had to beware lest desperadoes jump their claims, steal their gold, and kill them as they slept. To provide some measure of law and order various vigilante committees were formed. The "guilty" were separated from the "innocent" with scant attention to evidence.

Those who clawed at the countryside for gold by day found others who reaped their wealth by night. More money was banked by calculating merchants than by prospectors. At exorbitant prices lonely men purchased drink, fun, and excitement. Sometimes they said or did something wrong and were found dead the next morning. The rainbow trail to California rarely led to a pot of gold. Yet thousands upon thousands took this trail. By 1850, free blacks who had come to California numbered 962 and in two years that figure almost doubled. At the end of the decade the black population had doubled again.

One of the first black Californians was Mifflin W. Gibbs, who at twenty-two arrived in San Francisco in 1850. Though Gibbs was legally an adult male, he had none of the rights of citizenship. The Monterey Constitutional Convention of 1849 had settled that matter. The delegates spent more time deciding whether to admit black migrants than they gave to any other topic. Delegates agreed that blacks were "the greatest calamity that could befall California." While they failed to halt their migration to the state, they made sure blacks did not enjoy the rights of citizens.

Before the delegates left for home, they had written into their constitution provisions for excluding blacks from serving in the militia or voting. Those from the mining districts were most emphatic in their bigotry. In 1852 the legislature passed a law prohibiting black testimony in court. This meant that a black person could not file a claim for his gold mine, since he could not obtain a legal document. It also meant that the black woman who was attacked, the black businessman who was robbed, or the black farmer who was cheated—none of them could swear out a legal complaint or bring a white criminal to court.

For Mifflin Gibbs this law presented a clear danger. Along with a black partner named John Lester, Gibbs had established a fancy-clothing store featuring garments and shoes from abroad. One day a white entered the store, took a pair of boots, struck Lester—who chased after him—and walked away a free man. There was nothing further the black proprietors could do.

But there was something that black Californians could do. A black Franchise League in San Francisco began a campaign against the testimony law. Petitions sent to the legislature were laughed at by the delegates though they contained signatures of blacks and whites. The black response was to intensify agitation against the law. In 1855, and during the next two years, black Californians met in conventions to denounce discrimination in general and the testimony law in particular. At the first convention delegates proposed a newspaper to unite the black community in its own defense. Mifflin W. Gibbs was chosen to head that project, and *Mirror of the Times* was soon being sold in thirty California communities from the Mexican border to the Oregon line.

Mirror of the Times sparked the reform campaigns and gave people a chance to express their views on a variety of subjects. Thomas Duff wrote in from Mariposa denouncing the state taxes imposed on blacks to pay for white schools "from which our children are excluded." Editorials in the paper urged blacks to surrender such positions as waiters, bootblacks, and servants, and to pursue instead the professions, farming, or mechanical trades.

The yearly state conventions of blacks attracted some of the best leaders in the fields of education, the ministry, and business. J. B. Sanderson, who established schools for blacks, was one delegate. His schools in Oakland, San Francisco, Stockton, and Sacramento trained young black people to read, write, and do arithmetic. William H. Newby, another delegate, was editor of *Mirror of the Times*. When a man suggested that the convention of 1856 "hail with delight" America's progress, he became furious. "I would hail with delight the advent of a foreign army upon our shores, if that army provided liberty to me and my people in bondage," he responded. No resolution hailing America with delight ever was passed by the black conventions of California.

Following each convention a new petition campaign was launched to repeal the testimony law. Mifflin Gibbs repeatedly rode throughout the state collecting signatures, organizing meetings, and then going to Sacramento to deliver the petitions to the California legislature. He later wrote: "We had friends to offer them and foes to move they be thrown out the window."

As a successful businessman Gibbs was subject to a poll tax even though he could not vote. When his firm refused to pay, California officials seized a large amount of his goods and put them up for sale to collect their tax. Gibbs promised he would never pay the tax no matter what the penalty. But a white friend came to his aid. When his goods were put up for auction by the government, he moved among the crowd urging people not to bid. There were no bids and the merchandise was returned.

By 1857, when the third black California convention met, events were moving swiftly against minorities. The Supreme Court had announced its Dred Scott decision denying blacks any rights that whites were bound to respect. Whites, frightened at the rising Chinese population, were hounding the Asians in their midst with restrictions and violence. The next year the state legislature again unsuccessfully tried to ban black migration. It still refused to repeal the testimony law so bitterly resented by the black community.

A black exodus out of California resulted from these adverse pressures. Many traveled to Fraser Valley, Canada, where a gold strike had taken place. Mifflin Gibbs joined the gold-seekers. In British Columbia he opened a store and soon entered politics. By 1866 he had been elected a councilman from a white district. Following an interest in law, he completed a law course at Oberlin College and in 1870 was admitted to the Arkansas bar. Three years later he was elected a city judge in Little Rock—the first elected black judge in American history.

He had risen high through his own efforts. Repeatedly he

tied his future to the needs of his people. He died in 1903, soon after he wrote his autobiographical *Shadow and Light*. From bootblack, merchant, and gold-seeker to newspaper publisher and judge—these were his achievements in a country that held his people down. His life inspired many young western blacks. ,

Mifflin W. Gibbs. His rise from bootblack to judge inspired many young western blacks.

CLARA BROWN

Leading Citizen of
Central City, Colorado

In 1859 when Clara Brown, an ex-slave, arrived by wagon train in Denver, the place was still called Cherry Creek. She was merely one of thousands who had packed up for Colorado after the discovery of gold in the eastern foothills of the Rocky Mountains. Eager men had paused only to print "Pike's Peak or Bust" on their Conestoga wagons before joining the mass of gold-hungry humanity.

Everyone had heard of the gold found in California a decade before, and of those who made a fortune at the diggings. As the nation moved toward civil war and found itself in the midst of a business depression, Colorado gold signaled economic opportunity to the young and daring. Prospectors, the unemployed, outlaws, and heads of families flooded into the region from east and west. Not all came for the gold. Many arrived to fleece those busy searching for the precious metal. There was a fortune to be made in serving or robbing those infected with "gold fever."

The "Fifty-Niners," as they were called, arrived in Colorado a hundred thousand strong by June 1859. Their tent camps spread out wherever they heard whispers about shining metals. Streams were panned, rocks were chipped, and holes dug into huge mountains. The newspaper stories the prospectors had read (or been told of) had only misled them with exaggerated tales of gold pieces spread on the mountains and in the streams. By the end of the summer, fifty thousand miners returned to their homes. Discouraged, disgusted, and poorer than before, they made their way back to their expectant families. Their wagons no longer carried the enthusiastic "Pike's Peak or Bust." Some carried the painful admission "Busted, by Gosh."

Clara Brown was one of those who remained in Colorado. She had not come to pan for gold but to find work among those who did. Life for her was not without its dangers in a frontier mining community. Men outnumbered women by ten to one or more. Law was homemade, and sometimes this meant some men granted themselves the shield of legal power the better to cheat others. In this situation a black woman had to be careful and gather friends who would stand by her.

The early towns of Colorado were often organized around saloons, and these were crowded with potentially dangerous men. Outlaws rode in and out of town with impunity, and shoot-outs and murders were common. Gamblers, desperadoes, and confidence men abounded, and a large number of the females were prostitutes imported from abroad or the major cities of the nation. Whites seized Indian lands and often shot Indians on sight, but they claimed to have brought "civilization" to the West.

While others were digging for gold or spending it foolishly in the saloons, Clara Brown was trying to bring law and order to the frontier. During her short stay in Denver in 1859 she

helped start the Union Sunday School that had been opened by
two white Methodist ministers. This building rarely attracted
those who needed its Christian message, but it did give solace
to those settlers and their children who wanted spiritual comfort.

Soon Clara Brown left Denver to seek work following the
rush of prospectors to Central City. Unloading her stove, tubs,
and washboilers, she set about establishing a laundry in the
mining camp. Some considered her charge of fifty cents for
cleaning a red flannel shirt high, but they were glad to have a
laundry, and paid the price. Had she charged less, she might
have argued, she would not have been able to support herself at
the inflated prices in the mining camps.

Miners found that her laundry was only one of Clara
Brown's contributions to their welfare. She had abilities as a
nurse, and so they turned to her when illness struck. As her
resources expanded, she turned her home into a refuge for
many pouring into the camp. It served as her hospital, church,
and hotel. Those who could not pay were not turned away.
Under her direction the camp's first Sunday school began
operating. Far and wide Fifty-Niners talked of "Aunt" Clara
Brown and her many helping ways.

Rarely did she mention her own problems, her melancholy
background, for she felt rescued from a terrible fate and thrust
into a joyous new one. Born a slave in Virginia in 1803, she
was only three when, with her mother, she was sold to another
owner. At eighteen she was married and found some happiness
despite her bondage. Then, when she was thirty-five, her master died and his estate was sold at auction. Her husband, her
daughters, and her son were sold to different owners and her
new master whisked her off to Kentucky. After she had been in
service twenty years, her new master died. But this time her
owner's three daughters helped to purchase her liberty. Clara
Brown contributed a hundred dollars she had been saving and

won her release from bondage. Clutching her precious freedom papers, she headed west to St. Louis. Kentucky law required any slave liberated on its soil to leave the state or face reenslavement. Free at fifty-five, she became a cook, but not for long. Hearing some mountain men discuss the latest gold strikes in Colorado, she asked if they could use someone to cook and wash for them. They agreed to take her and her laundry equipment in exchange for her services. She made the long journey in the back seat of a covered wagon in a carvan of thirty. During the eight-week trip she assisted with the sick and proved fearless during Indian battles, epidemics, and other dangers of the trail. By the time she arrived in Denver, Colorado, she had made two great resolves. First, she would become independent and prosperous, then she would use her money to find relatives separated from her by slavery.

When the Civil War ended, Clara Brown had achieved part of her objectives. She had accumulated ten thousand dollars, some of which was invested in Colorado property. She left for Virginia and Kentucky to search for relatives, and returned with thirty-four of them. She took them by steamboat to Leavenworth and then across country by wagon to Denver, where they settled. Then she helped other blacks come West.

Unfortunately she had not found her son or daughters. But finally a neighbor located a daughter, Eliza Jane, and the two were happily reunited. Clara Brown lived on in Denver until her death at eighty-two. "A story of Colorado might well be woven around the life of this noble woman," wrote one western historian.

Aunt Clara Brown did more than leave a legend and warm feeling in the hearts of those who knew her. After the Colorado Pioneers Association buried her with honors, her friends made sure that those yet to be born would know of her work. A plaque was placed in the St. James Methodist Church telling how her house was the church's first home. A chair in the

Opera House was named in her honor. She had come to Colorado not for instant wealth, but for a happy life. In time she accomplished what she wanted for herself and for others she considered less fortunate than herself.

Clara Brown aided blacks in Colorado. (DENVER PUBLIC LIBRARY WESTERN COLLECTION)

BARNEY FORD

✦

HENRY O. WAGONER

Gold Seekers, Businessmen, and Civil Rights Fighters

Barney Ford and the five other black men who had struck it rich just southeast of Breckenridge, Colorado, could not sleep one night in 1860 because of the Supreme Court. In its Dred Scott decision a few years earlier the high court had ruled that blacks did not possess the rights of citizens. This meant that Barney Ford and his five prospectors could not file their land claim.

They knew they had found a fine spot for gold and were determined to protect it. Ford finally asked a white lawyer if he would please file their claim under his name. The lawyer did, and as soon as the blacks struck it rich, insisted it was his land all along. The local sheriff arrived at the diggings with an order to vacate the land in twenty-four hours. The black men huddled together planning their next move. They could not attack either the Supreme Court's or the sheriff's order. Both were quite legal.

Suddenly the blacks heard hoofbeats and knew riders had come to speed their departure and seize their gold. Without food or blankets, the six fled. The whites searched for a secret supply of gold, but found none. They started a tale that somewhere in the mountain Ford and his friends had left it buried. Many a prospector tried to locate the gold, but none ever struck it rich at Barney Ford's claim.

However, for the next century that mountain was called "Nigger Hill." Until 1964 this was the only monument to Barney Ford in the state. It was less than a fit tribute for a legendary Colorado figure.

Together with his good friend Henry O. Wagoner, Ford had aided the economic and political growth of the region for over fifty years. The two black men had both begun their lives working in southern cotton fields. Ford was seventeen when he was told his slave mother had drowned while trying to locate an agent for the underground railroad to help him escape. When Ford finally did escape from slavery and came to Chicago, he met Wagoner for the first time. Both men had taught themselves how to read and write.

Their political and family life began to expand in Chicago. Wagoner became a correspondent for Frederick Douglass's newspaper, wrote for a local paper, and served as a stationmaster on the underground railroad. He soon drew Ford into the secret work of the underground railroad. He also introduced him to Julia, his sister-in-law, whom Ford eventually married.

Barney and Julia Ford set out for California when gold was discovered there. But when their ship stopped in Nicaragua, they decided to try their luck in the hotel business. The United States Hotel, hosted by the adventurous couple, entertained

Barney Ford. (DENVER PUBLIC LIBRARY WESTERN COLLECTION)

American and foreign dignitaries. By the time they returned to Chicago, the Fords had made five thousand dollars and a lot of friends.

When the Colorado gold rush beckoned, Ford again answered. This time he made it to Denver City, only to be refused passage on a stagecoach because he was black. He took a job as a barber on a wagon train heading toward the gold fields. At Mountain City he again faced discrimination. Barred from a hotel because of his color, he had to board with Clara Brown. Even when he finally got to the diggings and began working, whites jumped his claims.

After the disaster at "Nigger Hill" in 1860, Ford abandoned

Henry O. Wagoner. (STATE HISTORICAL SOCIETY OF COLORADO)

prospecting for Denver and a calmer life. With Wagoner he
opened a string of business enterprises—barber shops, restau-
rants, and hotels. Ford's Inter Ocean Hotels in Denver and
Cheyenne catered to Presidents and prospectors, and offered a
wide variety of services from saloons to shaving. The establish-
ments had a reputation as far east as Chicago for "the squarest
meal between two oceans." When fires three times gutted their
premises, Ford and Wagoner each time were able to begin
anew.

After the Civil War, Colorado's constitution still prohibited

Ford's Inter-Ocean Hotel in Denver was just one of his many enterprises.
(DENVER PUBLIC LIBRARY WESTERN COLLECTION)

blacks from voting. Ford felt discouraged and took his family
back to Chicago, where black people had more rights. But
Wagoner pleaded with him to go to Washington and lobby
against the discriminatory parts of the Colorado statehood bill,
which was then pending. Ford met and discussed the matter
with Senator Charles Sumner, who was then able to maneuver
elimination of the prohibition against black voting rights. Again

the Fords returned to Denver and a reunion with their friends.

In Wagoner's home, Ford and a group of prominent black citizens started Colorado's first adult education classes. Black people were taught reading, writing, arithmetic, and the principles of democratic government. The program was a success.

In time Ford became the first black man to serve on a Colorado grand jury. Wagoner became the first black to serve as a deputy sheriff in Arapaho County, Colorado. In honor of their contribution to Colorado's early history, Barney and Julia Ford became the first blacks invited to a dinner of the Colorado Pioneers Association.

The Fords and Wagoner won a place in Colorado hearts and history. When the definitive *History of the State of Colorado* was published in 1895, more than two pages were needed to tell of Ford's part in the making of the state. His section was larger than that of several governors and other prominent whites. But the writer of his biography neglected to mention what Ford never forgot—that he was a black man. Later editions of the book replaced Ford's photograph with a picture of a white man. Finally, in 1964, "Nigger Hill" became "Barney Ford Hill" on local maps of the area.

WILD, BAD,
AND GOOD
COWPUNCHERS

BOSE IKARD

Faithful Cowhand on the
Goodnight-Loving Trail

The Civil War was over, leaving 600,000 Americans dead and many more wounded. But the industrial growth sparked by the demands of war remained. A rapidly expanding population wanted beef, and black, white, and Mexican trail crews drove cattle from Texas up the Chisholm Trail to northern rail junctions. By 1867, Abilene, Kansas, had become the first great cow town. It was able to load forty cattle cars in two hours, and so cattle poured into Abilene.

The long drives from Texas brought a million head of cattle to northern railroad terminals. Some single herds were as large as 15,000, though all agreed that 2,500 was the most manageable number. Bigger herds were more easily stampeded, this led to the death of hundreds of animals and the loss of all profit.

The average trail crew for the two- or three-month journey numbered eleven men. It was governed by the trail boss who by common agreement was given absolute power. He made the key decisions; often he owned the cattle. A herd of steers traveled up to fifteen miles a day, but the rate was much slower for cows. Driving cattle too fast meant a loss in weight that substantially reduced the herd's value in Kansas.

The cowboys worked as a team and depended upon one another's skills. Life on the trail was alternatingly exciting, dangerous, and dull. Above all it was hard and tedious work, having little to do with the glamour given it by movies and western novels. When they reached Abilene, the trail crew members received their pay of a hundred dollars or less and rode off to spend it.

Though Americans have come to think of cowboys as looking something like John Wayne or Gregory Peck, many looked like Sammy Davis, Jr., or Sidney Poitier. About a third of the 35,000 men who drove cattle northward were either black or Mexican. The typical trail crew had two or three blacks among its eight cowboys. Even if until recently these blacks never rode across the movie screens or pages of western novels, they did ride the western trails.

Blacks were among those spending long hours in the saddle keeping the herd together, and among those swallowed up by stampedes or rampaging rivers. Some froze to death and others were killed by wild animals. But most survived, sat around each night eating their grub, thinking of what might come next. Few got into conflicts with other members of the trail crew. They were hazed, like all new men, and some whites found their presence upsetting. But blacks generally turned a deaf ear to white anger.

In town it was a different matter. Released from the labor and restraints of the long drive and flushed with money, blacks and whites alike flooded the saloons, dance halls, brothels, and jails of the cow towns. As the first cow town, Abilene quickly gained a reputation for lawlessness. In 1870 when the town built a stone jail, cowboys pulled it down. When rebuilt, the jail's first customer was a black Texan who had shot up the town. He had not hit anyone, but made a lot of noise. His black and white trail crew took his arrest badly. They rode into Abilene, drove the marshal into hiding, and raided the jail to release their friend.

Ambitious Texas cattlemen wanted more trails northward than the Chisholm Trail to Abilene. Charles Goodnight and Oliver Loving sought a more westerly route north to New Mexico, Colorado, and Wyoming. Their most reliable cowpuncher was Bose Ikard, born a slave in Mississippi in 1847 and brought to Texas when he was only five. At the end of the Civil War, Ikard, who had learned to ride, rope, and fight near Weatherford, was hired by Oliver Loving and Charles Goodnight. In 1866 they founded the Goodnight-Loving trail.

It was always a dangerous trip. Empty wastelands, hostile Comanches, and sparse water holes confronted them. Loving died in a Comanche battle, but Goodnight and Ikard continued the partnership. Later Goodnight told how Ikard's devotion had saved his life several times. Although they buried Loving with an Indian arrow in him, they learned to respect the natives of the Southwest. They tried to avoid conflict if they could, but were prepared for battle when inevitable.

Goodnight always recalled Ikard with respect and affection: "He surpassed any man I had in endurance and stamina. There was a dignity, a cleanliness, and a reliability about him that was wonderful. He paid no attention to women. His behavior was very good in a fight, and he was probably the most devoted man to me that I ever had." Ikard was only one of many black and white cowpunchers who made up the Goodnight trail crew.

In the uncertain days of the Old West, Ikard served a valuable function for Goodnight. "I have trusted him farther than any living man. He was my detective, banker, and everything else in Colorado, New Mexico, and any other wild country I was in." When the two bedded down at night, it was Ikard who carried the money on his body. "I gave it to Bose," said Goodnight, "for a thief would never think of robbing him—never think of looking in a Negro's bed for money." It was a clever tactic, depending on people's racial stereotypes, and it worked.

For four years the two men endured every hardship on the trail together, fending off death in stampedes and Comanche raids, suffering through drought and lack of food. Cheerful, willing, and resourceful, Ikard was also "the most skilled and trustworthy man I had." In 1929 when Ikard died and was buried in Weatherford, Goodnight put up a marker over his companion's grave. It spoke of the cowpuncher's "splendid behavior," the loyalty of a man who "never shirked a duty or disobeyed an order."

DEADWOOD DICK
(NAT LOVE)

Wild Man
of the Old West

The West was filled with "wild men," cowboys off on a spree after the long drives up the Chisholm and other trails. Loaded with liquor and their wages, they roared into town and "had a good time." The town folk were usually happy when they left, even the storekeepers who made money on their trade. Sometimes cowpuncher antics got out of hand and caused pain or death, and a few had to be hauled off to boot hill for burial. But in their untamed way, they helped build the West, giving it their labor and their lusty appetites, and taking from it precious little in money or land.

One of the wildest men of the western trails was Deadwood Dick, hero of a nickel novel first published in 1877. No one knows who the original Deadwood Dick was, if there was a single mold at all. But one of those later to claim the title was an ex-slave from Tennessee called Nat Love. His home state did little for the freedmen following the Civil War, and this black teen-ager could not even find a school to attend. White supremacy ruled in the South and so Nat Love decided to head west.

Most of what follows comes from Love's own story, *The Life and Adventures of Nat Love, Better Known in the Cattle Country as "Deadwood Dick,"* written in 1907, and filled with tales of his great feats. He rarely understated anything, especially his own courage, power, and accomplishments. His book tells of "an unusually adventurous life."

In 1869 he arrived in the bustling town of Dodge City, Kansas, "a typical frontier city, with a great many saloons, dance halls, and gambling houses, and very little of anything else." Dodge City apparently drew no color line, so that Love and other black cowpunchers were accommodated on the same terms as whites—"as long as our money lasted." The ex-slave landed a cowboy job at thirty dollars a month and was nicknamed "Red River Dick." For the next twenty years or so he took part in the long drives that guided Texas beef up the trails for shipment to points east and west.

He was adopted by an Indian tribe that captured him after a furious battle. To escape he had to ride twelve hours on an unsaddled horse. One time he tried to rope and steal a United States Army cannon. His good friend Sheriff Bat Masterson got him out of that scrape. Another time he rode his horse into a Mexican saloon and ordered two drinks—one for him and one for his horse. Are these stories true? Maybe, and they make interesting reading.

Love spins his tales in typical boastful western fashion, detailing almost unbelievable instances of his personal bravery. In his first fight with Indians he initially "lost all courage." After he fired a few shots, however, he "lost all fear and fought like a veteran." From then on one danger was conquered after another. Love is the self-made frontier hero, proud and loud. At

Nat Love, better known as Deadwood Dick.

times he sounds more like a dime-store version of a western hero than a flesh-and-blood cowpuncher. While some might prefer him less of a braggart and more restrained, this was not his nature or writing style. With obvious relish and calm self-assurance, he fought wild animals and men and lived to tell the tale in his own way.

Throughout, Love is invincible. On his first job he broke in "Good Eye," the wildest horse in the corral. At one point he writes, "I carry the marks of fourteen bullet wounds on different parts of my body, most any one of which would be sufficient to kill an ordinary man, but I am not even crippled." Nat Love was no ordinary man. At another time he relates, "Horses were shot from under me, men killed around me, but always I escaped with a trifling wound at the worst."

Living the rugged cowpuncher life made a man of Nat Love. Some of his harrowing experiences would have sent others scampering back east. But fearless Nat Love could say, "I gloried in the danger." He tells of the western code for men: "There a man's work was to be done, and a man's life to be lived, and when death was to be met, he met it like a man." Tenderfeet could never measure up to this western standard.

Riding the range with Love were many other black cowpunchers. However, Love tells nothing about discrimination out west, and he must have been both victim and witness to some. He fails to mention any distinction made by anybody on the basis of race. From Billy the Kid to the Spanish maiden who was his first passion, no one seems bothered by his color. No one mentions it, and he seems to have forgotten it himself.

On the other hand, Love's attitudes toward other nonwhites are identical with the stereotypes held by whites at the time. Mexicans are "greasers," not to be trusted, and unclean. Indians are "terrorizing the settlers . . . defying the Government." He has little use for either group, no more than whites of this era had. Many cowpunchers also felt the same way about blacks, but this is not referred to.

On July 4, 1876, Nat Love entered the rodeo at Deadwood City in the Dakota Territory. He won some roping and shooting contests, and something more valuable: "Right there the assembled crowd named me 'Deadwood Dick' and proclaimed me champion roper of the Western cattle country." This great honor Nat Love carried with him for the rest of his life. To preserve it for posterity, he made it part of the subtitle of his autobiography. He was the only black cowboy to write a full-length book on his western experiences.

The railroad finally caught up with Deadwood Dick and the rest of the cowboys driving cattle up the trails. By shipping the cattle by rail, valuable pounds of beef were saved. The long drives were costly and time-consuming. Now they were unnecessary, because huge locomotives could quickly carry Texas beef to eastern and western markets. The trail crew was replaced by the galloping iron horse of progress.

In 1890 Nat Love left the range. He had to seek new employment, for he was still a young man and wanted a family. He took a job as a Pullman porter, one of the few jobs open to blacks of that era. In his new uniform he roared swiftly across the same lands he had roamed as a cowpuncher. He did not mind the work and he liked the tips. Perhaps this was because he had no choice.

He never forgot those great days on the range when work was hard, dangerous, and satisfying. And he never forgot his soul mates Bat Masterson, Frank and Jesse James, Billy the Kid, and others from both sides of the law.

BEN HODGES

He Made Dodge City
a Little Trickier

The story of Ben Hodges tells much about Dodge City, and the story of Dodge City reveals why men like Ben Hodges found it a satisfying place to live.

As Abilene faded in importance as a cattle town, the importance of Dodge City grew. By 1872 it was booming. It was more than just a shipping point from which Texas beef was whisked to eastern consumers. It was the end of a long, dry trail for thirsty men. During the day it was a dull, drab hamlet, its dusty streets needing wooden planks to walk on when rain turned the dust to thick mud. But at night, when trail crews rode in, it blossomed. Music and gaudy women overflowed its many saloons, dance halls, and brothels. Thieves, rustlers, highwaymen, card sharks, and con men played on the innocent consumers—skilled cowpunchers searching for fun and some excitement.

Dodge was the Wild West. Good men, bad men, black men, and white men shot it out on its streets. Some bore a grudge, but others merely thought it would be fun to fire into the air. The first man killed in Dodge was a black cowboy named Tex. Like everyone else in the crowd that day, he just came out to watch the gunfight between two whites. A stray bullet took his life.

Efforts to bring law and order to Dodge met with dismal failure. A vigilance committee of prominent merchants was able for a time to frighten off desperadoes. Then it was infiltrated by the men it sought to expel. It took U.S. Army troops to drive the new vigilance committee from Dodge. Dodge citizens hired men like sheriffs Wyatt Earp and Bat Masterson to handle criminals, and these men made sure guns were checked before people entered public places. This also gave the lawmen a decided advantage in the omnipresent card games. Only the marshal was armed, and every player knew this.

Ben Hodges, son of a black father and Mexican mother, rode into Dodge City with one of the first trail crews. He rarely left thereafter, lived a long and criminal life, and died from natural causes in 1929. Although he loved Dodge, the residents entertained mixed feelings about him. And with good reason.

To Ben Hodges life was a series of opportunities to gain something for nothing. He found that if he kept enough people laughing at his antics and only aimed his schemes at the wealthy, he could keep his enemies in disarray. His plans generally worked, and even when they fell through, he found he had lost little since it was other people's fortunes he was toying with.

When Hodges heard that a large land grant near Dodge belonged to an old Spanish estate, he went into action. In Texas he gathered documents claiming him as the legitimate owner of the land. With great sincerity he carried on his hoax, aided increasingly by residents who knew his claim was a phony. If he won, they figured, they would all gain. His prestige rose and with it the number of people willing to grant him credit. Soon the president of the Dodge City National Bank, a newcomer in town, extended him credit and a letter affirming his right to large sections of Kansas land. On this basis he tried to buy cattle on credit, but this scheme failed. However, each year the railroads, convinced he was a prosperous cattleman, granted him free passes.

The only two photographs of Ben Hodges show a determined man holding a shotgun and carrying six-guns. These pictures do him a grave injustice. Although he did use his guns when rustling, he really relied more often on his wits and talents as a forger, liar, and cheat. Whether he was a good shot is not known. But all reports placed him among the master fast-talkers and con men of Dodge, and in this area the competition was almost as great as that among fast gunslingers.

One day the law finally caught up with the smooth showman. He was arrested for stealing a herd of cows, and the evidence was damning. By now his reputation was known; he had little money, and had to plead his own case. The heavy betting was against acquittal. Ben Hodges talked to the jury for two hours. He had them straining to hear his every word, and laughing when he wanted them to. This was the core of his defense:

What me, the descendant of old grandees of Spain, the owner of a land grant embracing millions of acres, the owner of gold mines and villages and towns situated on that grant of which I am sole owner, to steal a miserable, miserly lot of old cows? Why, the idea is absurd. No, gentlemen, I think too much of the race of men from which I sprang, to disgrace their memory.

Later he contradictorily said that he was only a poor cowboy set upon by vicious foes. Still, the jury found Hodges not

Ben Hodges used his wits more than his guns. (DENVER PUBLIC LIBRARY WESTERN COLLECTION)

guilty. The stolen cows wandered home a few days later from the canyon where he had hidden them, but the case was now closed.

Those who played cards with Ben Hodges and those who only knew him by reputation were given a start one day. He wanted to become Dodge's livestock inspector, and they were sure that the governor would never appoint the fox master of the henhouse. When his petition, signed by gamblers, prostitutes, and unwary newcomers, reached the governor, the town's businessmen sprang into action. They pointed out to the governor that although Hodges was a loyal Republican, as his petition stated, he was also a leading cattle thief. His petition was rejected and Hodges went back to playing poker with his friends.

When Hodges died, his body was carried up to the Maple Grove Cemetery by some of his buddies. There it was laid to rest among the other cattlemen and cowboys of Dodge. "We buried Ben there for a good reason," explained one of the pallbearers. "We wanted him where they could keep a good eye on him." Hodges had survived lawless years, making his own inimitable contribution to the disorder of the town he loved.

CHEROKEE BILL

The Worst Man
in the West

In the western lands where violence became a way of life many a young man tried to prove his manhood through his gun barrel. It was considered something of an honor to be feared. Sometimes men shot it out and died over their claim to being "best shot" or "most feared" man in town. In time Americans from the East and West were caught up in a debate over who was the worst outlaw, the most accurate gunman, the most feared desperado.

These dubious distinctions have been granted to Billy the Kid. All agree he was the worst. Many writers have told tales of this ugly, buck-toothed psychopathic killer who was born in New York City in 1859 as Henry McCarty (he may have lived under the name William H. Bonney). The only photograph of him shows a shabbily dressed young man with a vacant (if not imbecilic) look peering uncertainly into the camera. This outlaw, who died before he was twenty-two, after a string of murders, has become an American legend. Actor Robert Taylor played Billy the Kid when Hollywood made a movie of his life.

By contrast, Cherokee Bill, no less a murderer, has faded from history. However, at least one man was ready to state that Cherokee Bill was the worst he had ever seen. Judge Isaac Parker, the famous "hanging judge" of the Old West, who sent seventy-nine men to their death on the scaffold, found Cherokee Bill without peer in the world of western desperadoes. The judge told the young man, "You are undoubtedly the most ferocious monster, and your record more atrocious than all the criminals who have hitherto stood before this bar." Like Billy the Kid, Cherokee Bill would surrender his life to violence at an early age.

Born Crawford Goldsby in 1876, Cherokee Bill began life in an atmosphere of law and order. His black father and Indian-and-white mother brought up the child on the military reservation of Fort Concho, Texas. Mr. Goldsby was a trooper in the famed Tenth Cavalry that policed the frontier. Young Goldsby received some education in Kansas and then at an Indian Catholic school in Pennsylvania. His behavior was considered normal until that point.

Then conditions at home changed rapidly. His mother left his father and later remarried. The new husband and the boy clashed. Bill as a teen-ager began to team up with "bad company." He left home and struck out for himself, remembering his mother's advice, "Stand up for your rights; don't let anybody impose on you." He worked in a store in the Oklahoma Territory and got in a few fights. Each battle seemed to give him an ever tougher attitude toward life and people. At eighteen he had his first shoot-out, wounding a black man who had beaten him in a fist fight.

For a time Cherokee Bill served as a scout for the Cherokee, Creek, and Seminole nations. This accounts for his ability to

*Cherokee Bill led
a short, violent life.*

ride through the Indian lands when escaping a posse, something his many pursuers could not do.

Cherokee Bill killed railroad agents, policemen, storekeepers, and in general those in his way. He killed without regard to whether his victims were armed or unarmed. Women found him attractive, and Cherokee Bill found women wherever he went. While visiting his favorite girlfriend, Maggie Glass, her cousin, Ike Rogers, who planned to turn him in for a reward, hit Bill on the head with a poker. Rogers turned him over the the law—and this meant Judge Isaac Parker. In sentencing Cherokee Bill to die, the judge expressed his personal view that execution was too good for him.

On the afternoon of a March day in 1896 Cherokee Bill was taken from his cell to the gallows. He was only twenty. Shortly before he left his cell he had told a friend how he used a rapid-fire technique to rattle his foes. This clever method, though it lacked accuracy, kept his enemies off balance and unable to make accurate shots themselves. Talk of guns and fighting were still important to him on this, the last day of his short life. Many agreed with Judge Parker's statement that here was " a human monster from whom innocent people can expect no safety."

The execution of Cherokee Bill brought his mother and a vast crowd to the prison yard. Since only a hundred tickets were given out, many others climbed over fences to witness the event. Calmly viewing the crowd, Cherokee Bill said, "Look at the people, something must be going to happen." His mother told him to keep up his courage, but she need not have offered the advice. Cherokee Bill was cool and collected to the end.

He obeyed a request to stand directly over the trap. Asked if he had any last words, he replied, "I came here to die, not to make a speech." The trap was then sprung and Cherokee Bill died in the kind of violence he had helped create.

His violent ways lived on. Ike Rogers, the man who had turned him over to the law, kept his gun. But not for long. At Fort Gibson, as he was descending a train, he was shot down by Cherokee Bill's brother, Clarence. Seizing the gun from the dying man, Clarence then fled on another train, firing at local officers as he did.

Even though Cherokee Bill was dead, his gun continued to deal death.

ISOM DART

He Tried Mightily
to Go Straight

Isom Dart was one of those many young men who spent his life as an outlaw trying to "go straight." He never made it. Born Ned Huddleston into slavery in Arkansas in 1849, the young boy was taken further south by his master during the Civil War. As a teen-ager he served a group of Confederate officers as an orderly, cook, and nurse. The hungry officers repeatedly sent him out to forage for chickens, fruit, and anything tasty he could find in the countryside. The young man soon came to enjoy this part of his work. For a slave it offered a lot more adventure and independence than serving men at a table.

With Emancipation he made his way to Texas and then Mexico. He picked up odd jobs, once as a clown in a rodeo. He teamed up with a Mexican and soon the two were stealing horses and swimming them across the Rio Grande in order to sell them to Texas cattlemen. They settled at Brown's Park in Colorado, a rugged country that had become a haven for cattle thieves. This northwest corner of Colorado touched the borders of Wyoming and Utah.

Dart tried his hand at prospecting for a time, but a partner cheated him and then drove him off their joint claim. He teamed up with a Chinese cook and the two played poker for profit. But then one night Dart lost heavily, the cook mysteriously vanished, and Dart was arrested on suspicion of murder. In jail he confronted the man who had driven him off the mining claim and again lost in a bloody fight. The next day he was released when the Chinese cook turned up alive and well.

Isom Dart decided to give up rustling and other illegal activities. He took a construction job and then turned to breaking in wild horses. At bronco-busting he had few peers. "No man understood horses better," wrote one westerner. Another added, "I have seen all the great riders, but for all around skill as a cowman, Isom Dart was unexcelled. . . . He could outride any of them; but never entered a contest."

Then love in the form of an Indian woman came into his life, and as quickly went out again. The experience left him bitter, and he returned to Brown's Park and a life of rustling cattle. In 1875 he joined the Tip Gault gang, which included his old Mexican partner. Though they stole cattle and horses, they did it for excitement rather than profit. One time when they were scouting a herd heading toward Wyoming, one of the gang was badly injured. That night Dart agreed to leave the others and help the wounded man. For a day and a night he remained with his dying companion, and then dug his grave.

As he lowered the man into the grave, he heard shots from the Tip Gault camp. He realized that a surprise attack had been made on his partners. With food, whiskey, and water he spent the night in the grave alongside his dead friend. He returned to camp to find the gang had been slain. He promised himself he

Isom Dart had few peers at bronco-busting. (DENVER PUBLIC LIBRARY WESTERN COLLECTION)

would go straight, change his name from Ned Huddleston to Isom Dart, and head farther west.

But eventually Dart drifted back to Brown's Park and then to rustling. And this time the law caught up with him. A deputy sheriff noted for his toughness headed toward Brown's Park with a warrant for Dart's arrest on charges of stealing cattle. During the journey back the deputy's buckboard crashed into a canyon. Dart, who was unhurt, aided the deputy, who had been knocked unconscious. After tending to his wounds, he lifted the buckboard onto the road, hitched it to the horses, and drove the deputy to the local hospital. Then he turned himself in at the local jail.

At his trial, the deputy testified to Dart's praiseworthy conduct. The jury agreed such behavior was proof of innocence and freed the black rustler. Dart rode back a new man to Brown's Park. He caught and broke wild horses, befriended local children, and soon had a ranch of his own.

Dogging the trail of rustlers was a bounty-hunter and gunslinger known as Tom Horn. He devoted himself to locating, warning, and then murdering from ambush rustlers who did not clear out of his way. He left a warning for Isom Dart and his partner, Matt Rash. But Rash was about to get married, and Dart at fifty-one had no intention of fleeing his peaceful life and ranch. Horn gunned Rash down as he ate breakfast.

Dart, though frightened, remained at his ranch surrounded by friends. One morning as he walked out of his cabin with two friends, a bullet from Horn's Winchester rifle ended his life. Good friends and some children mourned this black cowpuncher who had tried to go straight but could not escape his outlaw past. Three years later Tom Horn killed once too often. He was hanged for the cold-blooded murder of a fourteen-year-old boy.

Isom Dart had lived the dangerous life of a western badman. He had stolen property and killed men, and was therefore no different from many other outlaws who were swallowed up in violence. But the testimony on him is confusing. The soft words of those who knew him tell of a decent fellow. One man spoke of him as a "laughing sort of guy," and another as "a good man, always helpful." Finally, one woman recalled, "I remember Isom as a very kind man. He used to baby-sit me and my brother when Mother was away or busy." This also was Isom Dart, dead at fifty-one with a bullet in his heart.

Isom Dart (center right) with a group of cowboys in Brown's Park.
(DENVER PUBLIC LIBRARY WESTERN COLLECTION)

BILL PICKETT

The Greatest Cowboy
of the Day

From the days of slavery, blacks developed a tradition of handling horses. Black jockeys, stableboys, and trainers of horses were respected by their owners and other southerners. The extent of this tradition surfaced during the first Kentucky Derby, held in 1875. When the fourteen horses and their jockeys lined up at Churchill Downs, the betting was heavy. Hardly anyone was willing to bet that the first man across the finish line would be white. Why bet against the odds? Thirteen of the fourteen jockeys were black, and one of them was sure to win, and did.

For the rest of the century blacks continued to dominate the Kentucky Derby. Ike Murphy, who began racing horses at fourteen, had won forty-nine of fifty-one races in Saratoga by 1882. At Churchill Downs he became the first man to win the Kentucky Derby three times. In 1901 and 1902 Jimmie Winkfield won the Derby, the last of his race to do so. After this, black boys who wished to follow in the footsteps of Murphy and Winkfield found their path blocked. Horse racing had become big business. The whites who held the purse strings demanded that whites also hold the reins of the horses.

But out West the black tradition in handling horses flourished in rodeos. Cowboys had always enjoyed using their skills in competitive contests. At first it was all for fun, to see who could ride a bronco longest or rope a steer quickest. With the coming of rodeos at the turn of the century, these cowboy competitions turned into show business. The huge 101 Ranch in Oklahoma owned by the three Miller brothers, with its two hundred cowboys and a hundred thousand acres, put on one of the best rodeos in the West.

Starting with a grand parade of Indians, cowboys, and farmers, and ending with automobiles, the 101 Ranch Rodeo included a buffalo chase, Indian sports and dances, female riding stunts, bucking broncos, steer roping, a reenactment of an Indian attack on a Conestoga wagon, and a finale of singing "Home Sweet Home." From beginning to end it held the attention of its audiences. The rodeo was invited to perform in Chicago, New York, London, and Mexico City.

No matter where the rodeo played, the star billing went to an act called bulldogging by a black cowhand named Bill Pickett. Bulldogging was another name for steer wrestling, a cowboy sport for the powerful and strong in heart. But Pickett, an ex-slave, developed it to a high art and gave it a few twists that have forever stamped him as the inventor of modern bulldogging.

Pickett's special brand of bulldogging began innocently enough one day in Taylor, Texas. He was loading steers onto a stock car when one unruly animal turned back. Pickett turned his horse Spradley and galloped after the steer. Instead of trying to halt the beast, he leaped from his horse onto the steer,

Bill Pickett was the first black cowpuncher admitted to the National Rodeo Hall of Fame in Oklahoma City.

grabbing a horn in each hand. Next he twisted the animal's neck until it turned over on the ground on its side. This was unlike other efforts at bulldogging in that Pickett had not used a lariat—only his bare hands. He tried out his technique on other steers, and it worked each time. As a rodeo star Pickett honed his act to a fine point. His sense of timing, guts, and power gave it a flowing quality associated with a ballet performance.

Though he had practiced his act many times, the unexpected could always happen. The first time the 101 Ranch Rodeo came to Madison Square Garden in New York City performers and audience were in for a surprise. The steer Pickett planned to bulldog became frightened by the large crowd. It crossed the long arena and plowed into the grandstand. People screamed and scattered. Pickett followed in hot pursuit astride Spradley and bulldogged the steer in the stands. With his assistant, Will Rogers, who later became famous, he dragged the beast back into the arena. During the rest of its stay in the city the 101 Ranch played to a packed Madison Square Garden audience.

In 1908 the 101 Ranch rode into Mexico City during fiesta time, and the cowboys offered to demonstrate their skills. To insure a large attendance, boss Zack Miller announced Pickett would bulldog a fighting bull, or at least hold the raging beast for five minutes. There is no evidence to show that Pickett was consulted before the offer was made, but he did consent to try. Those who crowded the stand came to witness a killing, and almost had their wish.

When Pickett flew from his horse and gripped the bull's horns, he was in for the ride of his life. The bull whipped Pickett around, against walls, and tried to paw him loose. Angry that their bull has not shaken the cowpuncher, the fans began throwing bottles into the ring. One hit Pickett in the ribs and kept him from doing anything more than hold onto the bull for dear life. After six minutes the cowboys rushed into the ring to rope the bull and rescue their shaken hero. He had survived and his boss had won the bet.

In between rodeos Pickett worked at the 101 Ranch and saved up to buy his own ranch. In 1932 he was taking care of his old boss, Zack Miller, who had become ill. When he went to the corral to tend some horses for Zack, he was kicked by a sorrel. The seventy-year-old man fell and the horse stomped him, fracturing his skull. In eleven days Bill Pickett was dead.

The New York *Herald Tribune* reported the next day that from Madison Square Garden, where the circus was performing, to Wall Street, men were talking about this legendary cowboy and his bulldogging act. One of his old assistants, Will Rogers, who had become America's most admired comedian, wrote a letter to the New York *Times* about his likable, skilled buddy. "Even the steers wouldn't hurt old Bill," said Rogers. Another of Pickett's assistants in the 101 Rodeo had been Tom Mix, who also made the big time in radio and movies as a cowboy star. But Pickett, the cowpuncher Zack Miller described as "the greatest sweat and dirt cowhand that ever lived—bar none," soon faded from the memories of men.

In 1971 the historical record finally caught up with Bill Pickett's unique contribution to the West. The legendary "dusky demon" was admitted to the National Rodeo Hall of Fame in Oklahoma City, the first black cowpuncher to be accepted. A man responsible for one of those rare innovations that entertain millions and make history had finally received his due.

LAWMEN, SOLDIERS, AND SHAPERS OF THE FRONTIER

BASS REEVES

Bringing Law and Order
to Oklahoma

Shortly after three in the afternoon of January 12, 1910, people in the offices of the Muskogee, Oklahoma, federal courthouse were buzzing excitedly with the news. Many who had known Bass Reeves during his many decades as a deputy marshal were saddened by news of his death. They cheered themselves up with stories of his long, heroic career as a lawman in a lawless territory. It was a different Oklahoma now; a state in the Union, no longer a refuge for outlaws. Bass Reeves was a good part of the reason for that change.

Born a slave in 1840, Reeves grew to over six feet—a broadshouldered man of 180 pounds with large hands, muscular arms, and the will to use them against lawbreakers. In 1875 he began a career that would span the next thirty-seven years as a lawman in Oklahoma's Indian Territory. Even after his retirement in 1907, the year Oklahoma entered the Union, Bass

Bass Reeves. (WESTERN HISTORY COLLECTIONS, UNIVERSITY OF OKLAHOMA LIBRARY)

Reeves at sixty-nine found he could not quit. He joined the Muskogee police force for two years, until he had to retire because of illness.

The job of marshal was neither well-paying nor safe in Oklahoma when Reeves began. But once he mounted his sorrel horse and rode off to arrest a man, that man had little hope of getting away. In all his years as a marshal, Reeves is said to have failed only once to bring back his prey. That one time an outlaw named Hellubee Sammy, who lived near Boley, got on his swift black horse and outrode Reeves.

In a book published in 1901 on the Indian Territory, Bass Reeves is described as "the invincible deputy United States marshal," who once had to arrest two wagonloads of men for horse stealing. He also is said to have preached to his prisoners from time to time about the evils of a criminal life.

Although he was a dead shot with his revolver, Reeves boasted that he tried to avoid using it. He did admit to killing fourteen men in the course of his labors as a deputy marshal, but claimed no one had ever died at his hands unless he had drawn his gun on him first. All agreed that he had faced some of the most desperate and treacherous men in the territory, and had handled himself with courage and success.

During his long tenure as deputy marshal, Reeves served under seven United States marshals, and none of them ever complained about his work. Although he could neither read nor write, he managed to deliver stacks of subpoenas and keep his financial accounts in good order. His life was filled with excitement, and often great danger. He had a button shot off his coat, his belt shot in two pieces, his hat brim shot off, and his horse's bridle reins cut by bullets. He was never wounded—an outstanding and lucky record for so wild a land and job.

Reeves relied on both detective skills and disguises to snare his prey. To gain a $500 reward for catching two young men, he wore scuffed clothes and impersonated a tramp. He persuaded the mother of the boys to feed him and put him up until the boys returned. Then he convinced them he was a desperado. When the brothers fell asleep, he handcuffed them together and the next morning took them back to his camp. It was a twenty-eight-mile walk, and for three of the miles a furious mother dogged their trail screaming at the deputy marshal who had captured her sons.

Reeves was only one of many black marshals to patrol the Indian Territory. Many had lived their lives among Indians or among Indian freedmen, and so understood and appreciated Indian ways. This was not true of many white lawmen, and the Indians appear to have liked the black marshals better, perhaps because they felt a greater kinship with them and trusted them more. It is also likely that black lawmen made a greater effort to understand the native languages and ways. Reeves spoke the Creek language and perhaps others as well.

Bass Reeves was one of that lonely breed of lawmen who faced danger to bring order and justice to frontier communities. Their pay was low and the threat of death always hung over their lives. Yet they carried out their task with courage and ingenuity, and their successful efforts built a more civilized West.

POMPEY FACTOR

The Seminole Negro
Scouts of the U. S. Army

It is ironic that among those men who brought law and order to Texas after the Civil War was a band of black Indians who enjoyed neither law nor order. The Seminole Negro Indian Scouts, never numbering more than thirty at any time, faithfully served the U.S. Army as a crack scouting unit during the desperate 1870s on the Texas-Mexican border. They were rewarded with the hatred of white desperadoes and sheriffs; the failure of the government to honor its pledges of food, clothing, and land; and, finally, a casual termination from United States service after uncommon valor.

The Seminole Negro Indian Scouts were part of a proud fighting force that had helped defeat the United States in three Seminole Wars in Florida. Descendants of runaway slaves from Georgia, they had escaped to and lived among the Seminole nation in Florida. During a strenuous and successful effort to live a free, prosperous, and happy life, they had to battle United States slaveholder efforts to recapture them. Finally, after the last Seminole War in the 1840s, they agreed to leave for the West.

By then, though racially black, they spoke Spanish and a broken English, and had adopted the ways of the Seminoles. Most were Baptists. They had acquired and perfected the Seminole skills of trailing, hunting, and frontier combat, though they took to the warpath usually only in self-defense. Confined in the Indian Territory during the slave era, they were the target of slave catchers who kidnapped their women and children for sale in the southern states.

In disgust over this practice and the domination of the Creeks, several hundred black Seminoles left for Mexico. Wild Cat, an Indian, led one band, and John Horse, a black, led another. By 1870 slavery had ended in America, and the U.S. Army desperately needed trackers familiar with Indian ways and warfare. John Horse commanded 150 black warriors in southwestern Coahuila, and John Kibbett, his assistant, commanded another 100 not far from Eagle Pass, Texas. General Zenas R. Bliss of Fort Duncan, Texas, sent an emissary to contact Kibbett and hired his black Indians as United States scouts. An agreement by the two parties said that in return for scouting, the United States government would provide the scouts' families with food, travel expenses, and land grants in Texas.

On July 4, 1870, the Kibbett band arrived at Fort Duncan prepared to assume scout duties. The government provided the men with ammunition, rations, and carbines. The scouts provided their own horses. For whites they were a strange, if not terrifying, sight. Most wore Indian clothing, and some sported war bonnets that included buffalo horns. Repeatedly the military reports on the outfit praised the scouts' skills but con-

The Seminole Negro Indian Scouts were excellent hunters and trailers.

demned their clothing and appearance. They soon earned a reputation, General Bliss noted, as "excellent hunters, and trailers,
and brave scouts . . . splendid fighters." In tracking they had
no peers and were able to pick up a trail weeks old and cleverly
hidden by Indians skilled at concealing trails.

For the first few years they served under their own John Kibbett and were assigned to various infantry and cavalry units, both black and white. In 1873 a young Civil War veteran, Lieutenant John Bullis, was put in charge of the outfit. It was an excellent choice. Bullis had commanded black troops during the war and respected his men. He was a thin, wiry, short man with a black mustache and a face burned red from the Texas sun. For the next nine years he and his men participated in twenty-six expeditions, often against forces outnumbering them by six to one, and never suffered a death or severe wound.

The white officer and the black Seminole scouts developed a fine relationship. Bullis performed marriages in their village and visited families to bless newborn children. On the Texas plains he survived without rations when necessary. One can of peaches, corned beef, or corn a day was all he took "to be really luxurious" on marches. With his scouts he caught rattlesnakes and searched for water holes. He was known to those he tracked as "Thunderbolt" or "Whirlwind."

To his men Bullis was friend, guardian, and equal. Scout Joseph Phillips depicted the relationship in these words:

The Scouts thought a lot of Bullis. Lieutenant Bullis was the only officer ever did stay the longest with us. That fella suffer just like we-all did out in de woods. He was a good man. He was an Injun fighter. He was tuff. He didn't care how big a bunch dey was, he went into 'em every time, but he look for his men. His men was on equality, too. He didn't stand and say, "Go yonder"; he would say "Come on boys, let's go get 'em."

Bullis knew he could count on his soldiers in an emergency. On April 25, 1875, the young lieutenant had such an emergency. With Sergeant John Ward, trumpeter Isaac Payne, and Private Pompey Factor, Bullis attacked a party of thirty Comanches attempting to cross the Pecos River with seventy-five stolen horses. When the Comanches found out how few troopers there were, they counterattacked, firing their Winchesters. The Americans fled to their horses and began to gallop off. Sergeant Ward glanced back to see Lieutenant Bullis unable to mount his horse. Comanches swept toward the stranded officer. "We can't leave the lieutenant, boys," shouted Ward, and the three soldiers raced back. As Ward reached Bullis and lifted him onto his horse, a bullet cut his carbine sling. But that was the only mishap to befall the four.

Bullis later wrote, "I . . . just saved my hair by jumping on my Sergeant's horse, back of him." He saw that his three scouts received the Congressional Medal of Honor for their heroism.

The Seminole Negro Indian Scouts received little else from their government despite its promises. The pledged land grants were never made to their families. Instead they squatted on military reservations. Then the government halted rations to those who were not regularly enlisted scouts. This meant that more than two hundred people had to live on the food issued to fifty scouts. Women, children, and unemployed men became scavengers and thieves. Petitions by John Horse and John Kibbett were endorsed by three generals and Lieutenant Bullis, but to no avail.

In twelve major engagements, the outfit continued to inflict losses on their enemies without suffering death or serious casualties. "When you are fighting for the right and have your trust in God," said Scout Bill Daniels, "He will spread His hand over you." But no hand stayed the bigots in Texas who resented these skilled trackers. The King Fisher gang that dominated the Eagle Pass region shot it out with some of the scouts in a bar at Christmas in 1874. Another time the outlaws ambushed Chief John Horse and Titus Payne. Payne was killed immediately, but the old chief, despite a wound, managed to ride his horse into the Seminole camp.

For many of the Seminole Negro Indian Scouts the final

blow came in the early morning hours of a New Year's Eve
Dance at their reservation in 1877. A Brownsville sheriff came
to arrest Adam Paine, the fourth scout to earn the Medal of
Honor. Instead of making the arrest, the sheriff decided to
shotgun Paine, and from such close range that Paine's clothes
caught fire. This was the third murder of a scout in less than
two years. Pompey Factor and four other scouts rode to the Rio
Grande. There they paused to wash the dust of Texas from
their horses' hoofs and then they continued their journey into
Mexico, swearing never to return.

The other scouts remained, more loyal to Bullis and their job
than to the United States. Few of the older scouts reenlisted,
however, and their ranks were filled by discharged black troopers, Texas blacks, and Mexicans. The outfit continued effec-
tively to track and harass the red and white outlaws of the
region, and gradually drive them off. The borderlands near
Mexico finally became safe for families.

Bullis became a famous frontier fighter and later a brigadier
general in the U.S. Army. His Seminole Negro Indian Scouts
faded from view once their mission had been accomplished.
They became part of the dark poor of Texas and Mexico. They
had survived the Texas heat and dangers of the desert and had
not lost a man in savage combat. But they could not survive the
traditional racism of the U.S. Army or of white citizens, including those whom they had defended so courageously.

In 1926, Pompey Factor, by then an old man who could
hardly remember dates and other basic information, applied for
a pension. He could not prove he had been in the Army, but he
still held the Medal of Honor case that once housed proof of his
extraordinary heroism. Illiterate, feeble, but this time accom-
panied by two younger witnesses, he asked a lawyer in Brack-
ettville, Texas, to file his claim for a soldier's pension. Again,
his request was turned down.

Two years later, when he was in his eighties, Pompey Factor died and was buried in Bracketville alongside other black Seminole heroes at a cost of $86.40, paid by some unidentified citizen. Today his records have found their way into a file at the National Archives that prove Pompey Factor was indeed in the U.S. Army and did indeed earn the Medal of Honor, though he never was granted a pension to ease his final years.

Pompey Factor

HENRY ADAMS

Leading the Oppressed
to Kansas and Points West

The black man facing the Senate investigating committee looked directly at his questioners and answered them
in rapid-fire order. The senators wished to know what secret
plan was behind the vast black migration from the South in
1879. Southern whites, who depended on black labor, were
panicked. Democratic senators thought it was a Republican
conspiracy to move voteless blacks to the northern and western
states, where they could and would vote Republican.

Henry Adams knew something of freedom. Born a slave in
1843, he had been "hard at work all my life," and was liberated
during the Civil War. He joined the Army as a young man in
1866 and left it three years later. He returned to find that the
conditions facing blacks in freedom were almost as oppressive
as those they had faced as slaves. With others who had served
in the Army, where he had tasted a measure of dignity and lib-

erty, Adams formed a committee to determine if blacks "could stay under a people who had held us under bondage or not."

Calling the organization simply "the committee," Adams said they set out to "see whether there was any State in the South where we could get a living and enjoy our rights." For almost five years a hundred agents sent back written reports to the committee, and these were read at its meetings in Shreveport, Louisiana. Agents paid their own expenses, largely by working in the fields alongside the people they interviewed on their labor conditions.

Their reports told a dismal story of the lack of a true emancipation for southern blacks. "The people was still being whipped, some of them by the old owners, the men that had owned them as slaves, and some of them was being cheated out of their crops," Adams told the senators. If they tried to vote in certain states, "they would be shot" unless they voted for the Democratic party. In 1874 Adams's committee organized a "colonization council."

The President of the United States and Congress were contacted by the colonization council and asked "to help us out of our distress, or protect us in our rights and privileges." When nothing was done, another request was made "to set apart a territory in the United States for us." When that failed to draw a response, the council requested "an appropriation of money to ship us all to Liberia, in Africa; somewhere where we could live in peace and quiet." Finally, the council asked foreign nations to grant them a place to live. None of these pleas received any encouragement.

In 1877 when the last of the federal troops were withdrawn from the South, these black meetings were broken up by white mobs. Noted Adams, "We lost all hopes." After more meetings the decision was made to leave the South: "We said the whole South—every State in the South—had got into the hands of the very men that held us slaves . . . holding the reins of government over our heads in every respect almost, even the constable up to the governor. We felt we had almost as well be slaves under these men." A final appeal to President Hayes and both houses of Congress received no reply. By this time the council claimed membership of ninety-eight thousand.

Henry Adams and his council then led one of the largest mass migrations in western history. In the single year of 1879 an estimated twenty to forty thousand black men, women, and children left for Kansas and points west. Some traveled up the Mississippi River by river boat. Some made the long, slow walk up the Chisholm Trail. Most aimed to reach Kansas. They knew that John Brown had first struck against slavery on its broad plains, and they hoped to find good farming land to rent or buy.

The white South reacted with panic at the thought of losing its valuable laborers. Leaders of this "Exodus of 1879" were denounced and some were driven from towns or beaten. The Mississippi was closed to black migrants, with threats made to sink any boat carrying blacks northward. "Every river landing is blockaded by white enemies of the colored exodus," wrote General Thomas Conway to President Hayes. The whites were "mounted and armed, as if we are at war." A black who escaped to Kansas and returned South to get his family was seized by whites. His hands were cut off and he was thrown into his wife's arms with the comment, "Now go to Kansas to work."

But the "Exodusters" would not be halted, no matter how high the price in fear and blood. The United States senators learned, after 1,700 pages of testimony, that it was not a Republican conspiracy that drove blacks to Kansas, but southern oppression. One of the most interesting witnesses to follow Henry Adams with testimony before the Senate committee was tall, lean Benjamin "Pap" Singleton. As a slave he had tried to escape bondage a dozen times before he finally slipped into

A group of Exodusters at a Topeka, Kansas, fairground. (KANSAS STATE HISTORICAL SOCIETY)

Canada. He had been working on the migration since 1870, he told the senators. He also told them, "I am the whole cause of the Kansas migration." Historians would later credit Singleton with leading the Exodus of 1879.

The Exodusters who reached the West found that they had only traded one set of problems for another. Kansas relief facilities were so strained by the sudden arrival of so many penniless people that tragedy threatened. Kansans collected over a hundred thousand dollars for food, clothing, cooking utensils, and shelter for the ragged army from the South. Beef and money were sent from Chicago. Staffordshire pottery arrived from England. Miraculously, no one starved or froze to death that winter.

Western reception of penniless Exodusters was often friendly, but not always. A band of 150 Mississippi blacks was driven out of Lincoln, Nebraska. In Denver some residents refused to rent homes to the newcomers. But both of these angry responses eased in time. Blacks were soon graduating from Nebraska high schools, and Tom Cunningham became Lincoln's first black policeman. In Denver a group of black and white builders sold homes to the Exodusters on the installment plan.

In Nicodemus, blacks established a town that still stands. However, they had to spend their first winter in dugouts, unable to build homes until the spring. Bad luck dogged their early years. They faced repeated crop failures and finally had their crops blown away by a searing wind that left the rest of Kansas untouched. But, within less than a decade, the town prospered. It established churches, stores, lodges, a school, and two newspapers that sang its praises.

Many black western communities owe their birth to the pioneer work of Henry Adams, Pap Singleton, and their comrades. In the face of great odds and some danger, they tried to move a black population from southern oppression to freedom on the plains of America. Their success forms one of our great western sagas.

HENRY O. FLIPPER

✦

CHARLES YOUNG

The Black Military
Service in the West

From the earliest days on the frontier, whites have had very mixed feelings about arming blacks and have pursued a twisted path in admitting them to the armed forces. Although five thousand blacks served in George Washington's army and John Paul Jones's navy, they were admitted only after the British offered slaves freedom and a musket. First excluded from the Union army during the Civil War, hundreds of thousands of blacks came into the armed forces after Emancipation. Their presence may have meant the difference between victory and defeat for the Union, for they joined the Army at a time when both sides were running out of able-bodied men.

Their courage in the Civil War, with twenty-two blacks earning the Congressional Medal of Honor, led in 1866 to the formation of four black military units in the West. The Ninth

Cavalry and Tenth Cavalry constituted 20 percent of the entire U.S. Cavalry in the West. Commanded by white officers, they carried out the federal government's policy toward the Indian tribes. They helped crush the first victims of racism in America. Despite this, the black troopers served well, winning the respect of every military friend and foe they encountered. The Indians named them "Buffalo Soldiers," after an animal they considered sacred.

There were two black infantry regiments, the Twenty-fourth and Twenty-fifth. On the frontier, black soldiers thrived on the things that have always cushioned a lowly status: uniforms, loyalty to country, clean living quarters, skill development, and adherence to orders from above. If they were black mercenaries hired to carry out white genocide toward Indians, there is nothing, however, to indicate they saw their job that way.

From the Mississippi to the Rockies, from the Canadian to the Mexican border, the Ninth and Tenth patrolled. Their white scouts included the legendary Kit Carson and Wild Bill Hickok, and among their white officers was John J. Pershing, who earned the nickname "Black Joe" by leading the Tenth for several decades.

The black troopers found that headquarters regularly dealt them a bad hand. "This regiment has received nothing but broken-down horses and repaired equipment," complained Captain Louis Carpenter of the Tenth, one of five white officers to receive a Medal of Honor while leading black troopers. Black soldiers' punishments exceeded those given white soldiers, their stations were among the most isolated in the West, and their food and recreation left much to be desired. Even the Tenth's regimental flag was homemade, faded, and worn, unlike the silk-embroidered banners supplied to white regiments.

Even in the frontier towns they defended, the black soldiers found an icy and hostile reception. Jacksboro, Texas, with its two hundred white residents and twenty-seven saloons, had little to offer its black guardians. One citizen murdered a black soldier and then killed the two black cavalrymen who came to arrest him. A jury of his white peers found him innocent. Racial flare-ups and murders marked many a frontier town near a fort housing black soldiers. After an incident at El Paso, Texas, in 1900, Colonel James W. Hull, who commanded the Department of Texas, summarized the southern attitude: "A colored man in uniform represents authority, and this idea suggests superiority, which is bitterly resented."

Morale in black regiments, despite official and civilian animosity, remained higher than in white units. Black units had fewer courts-martial for drunkenness and fewer deserters. In 1876 the Ninth had 6 and the Tenth had 18 deserters. The white units had far more—the Third had 170, the Seventh (of George Custer) had 72, and the Fifth had 224. A black man joined not for adventure, as many whites did, but to secure a proud and decent job. He was not likely to surrender it because of adversity, animosity, or anger.

The courage of the Buffalo Soldiers became legendary on the plains. The Ninth Cavalry earned a reputation for always arriving in the nick of time to rescue settlers or other soldiers. The Tenth Cavalry made the first thorough exploration of Texas's Staked Plains, a trackless wasteland. For days they had to ride in temperatures of 100 degrees and over. Some eleven black troopers of the Ninth and Tenth earned the Congressional Medal of Honor. Artist Frederic Remington, who traveled on patrol with the Buffalo Soldiers, wrote this description of them:

The physique of the black soldiers must be admired—great chested, broad shouldered, upstanding fellows, with bull necks, as their rifles thrown across their packs they straddle along.

Sometimes the black troopers challenged the white hostility they found in towns. In 1878 Company D of the Tenth shot it

The Tenth Cavalry in Diamond Creek, New Mexico. (MUSEUM OF NEW MEXICO, R. SCHMIDT COLLECTION)

out in San Angelo near Fort Concho—their answer to the baiting and abuse heaped on them by the gamblers, prostitutes, and drunks in town. A Frederic Remington story and painting is based on this incident.

At West Point discrimination dogged the trail of the twenty black officer candidates admitted in the nineteenth century. Only three eventually graduated.

The first West Point black cadet was James W. Smith, admitted from South Carolina in the years following the Civil War. He found himself so harassed with "insults and ill treatment" by the other cadets that he could not concentrate. He was cursed and abused, and had trouble getting his share of food. When he finally struck back at his tormentors, hitting one on the head with a coconut dipper in the dining room, he was dismissed from the Academy.

The first black to graduate from West Point was Henry O. Flipper, son of a Georgia slave. In 1877 he survived the hostility of his classmates and instructors and graduated fiftieth in a class of seventy-six. His assignment to the Tenth Cavalry was brief. In a few years charges were brought against him for "embezzling public funds and conduct unbecoming an officer." The second charge grew out of the first. A court-martial found him innocent of the embezzling charge, but then managed to find him guilty of the second. The fact that while serving at Fort Concho, Lieutenant Flipper had taken a white woman riding might have had something to do with his dismissal.

Although dishonorably discharged from the Army, Lieutenant Flipper continued to enjoy the support of his government in many matters. Repeatedly he was hired as a civil engineer by the federal, state, and local Southwest governments. He was considered incorruptible and often hired to translate documents relating to Spanish land claims into English. The U.S. Senate Committee on Foreign Relations employed him as did the Secretary of the Interior. But Flipper was never able to win a new trial that would clear his military record.

Meanwhile racial relations at West Point had not progressed. Cadet Johnson C. Whittaker, after two years of academic success, was found tied to his bed, his ears and his hair cut. He was charged with inflicting the injuries on himself and court-martialed for blaming others. President Chester A. Arthur reviewed the case in 1882 and found that the evidence against Whittaker was insufficient. He sent the case back to the Academy's review board. Again, they decided against the young black cadet and dismissed him from service.

Lieutenant Henry O. Flipper, the first black graduate of West Point.

The last black cadet to graduate from West Point in the nineteenth century was Charles Young. "While West Point was pretty hard pulling for me," he wrote years later to a classmate, "still the roughness was relieved by the sympathy of many of my classmates. . . ." Graduating in 1889, Lieutenant Young was assigned to the Tenth Cavalry.

Young's military career spanned three decades, the longest of the three black graduates of West Point. During the Spanish-American War he commanded the black Ohio volunteers and took part in the charge at San Juan Hill. There members of the Buffalo Soldiers saved the day for the Rough Riders and Teddy Roosevelt.

During the Pancho Villa expedition into Mexico, Young served under John J. Pershing with the Tenth Cavalry. By the outbreak of World War I, Colonel Young thought his chance had come finally to lead black and white United States soldiers in the "war to make the world safe for democracy." He soon found out how wrong he was. The highest ranking black officer in United States history, he was suddenly dropped from active service. The official explanation was "high blood pressure." To disprove this excuse, he mounted his horse and rode from Ohio to Washington, D.C., and back. His effort was to no avail.

Not until three days before the armistice was he placed back on active duty. Soon he was assigned to diplomatic duty in Liberia, Africa. Much of his career and talents had been wasted. He had mastered six foreign languages and wrote poetry. He composed and played music for violin and piano. While on a visit to Nigeria in 1922 he contracted a fatal blackwater fever. After his death, his country took his body to Arlington National Cemetery for burial with full military honors.

The fate that befell the black cavalry and infantry units was also saddening. In 1906 President Theodore Roosevelt discharged many in the crack Twenty-fifth Infantry for shooting up the town of Brownsville, Texas. The accused soldiers denied they had been in town that night, and subsequent research has proven their innocence. In 1917 a battalion of the Twenty-fourth Infantry battled local citizens of Houston, Texas, killing seventeen and losing two of their own. The largest murder trial in American history followed, with many of the men being sentenced to death. Only a vigorous campaign by the NAACP convinced President Wilson to halt further prosecutions.

But the lesson of Colonel Young and the Buffalo Soldiers was unmistakable. Those who had fought to defend the frontier from intruders, and against the Spanish at San Juan and Pancho Villa in Mexico, had been hardly accorded their due. The Buffalo Soldiers had become scapegoats for white racism. Today the courage of the Ninth and Tenth Cavalry regiments lives on. An association of former members has been created. It holds conventions and issues news about the military tradition of these crack units.

EDWIN P. McCABE

Shaping a Black Dream in Oklahoma

Black Oklahoma

For red and black people, Oklahoma once loomed as a possible refuge from the onslaught of racism in America. The federal government had moved many eastern native societies there and spoke of it becoming an Indian sanctuary. But whites increasingly violated the Indian Territory, searching for fertile land and wealth. Then American blacks began to view Oklahoma as a possible black refuge.

The dream of a black Oklahoma in the Union was inspired by the personality of Edwin P. McCabe. In the twenty years following his arrival in the territory, some 25 black communities were formed, and the black population increased by 537 percent to 137,000. But the black dream, like the Indian dream, would fade with the arrival of white settlers, and their laws that crushed nonwhite political power. And Edwin P. McCabe would mysteriously disappear from the scene. His black followers would be divided as to whether the handsome young politician-nationalist had been slain by his enemies or had sold his people down the river.

McCabe was born in Troy, New York, in 1850, and attended schools in Massachusetts, Rhode Island, and Maine. His parents, though poor, urged him to continue his education and he did so until his father died. Then he was forced to leave school to support his mother, sister, and brother. After working on Wall Street in New York City as a clerk, he left for Chicago. Bright and educated, he secured a job in the Cook County Treasury. In 1874 he left for Kansas and when the Exodus of 1879 reached that state, he found himself a popular political leader in the black community. He was referred to by blacks and whites as "the recognized leader of his race in the West." In 1882 at a Republican convention of 394 whites and 6 blacks, he was nominated for state auditor. Winning the election made him the highest black elected official in the West.

Then his fortunes, his locale, and his views suddenly changed. At thirty-six, when he was not renominated, he left for California and then Oklahoma. He arrived at the time of the Oklahoma stampede of April 1889 when land was opened for settlement. Perhaps he may have found a new role for himself when he saw that of the thousands of eager folks lining up for the Oklahoma land rush, ten thousand were black. In Guthrie, McCabe found a man who sold him 160 acres, and then he bought another 160 acres. He established the McCabe Town Company and began sending agents into the South looking for prospective black migrants. He called his settlement Langston City, after the black lawyer who had just been elected a congressman from Virginia.

McCabe's agents had several powerful arguments in their promotion campaign. First, black southerners knew that lynchings were increasing and their rights were evaporating each

Edwin P. McCabe. (KANSAS STATE HISTORICAL SOCIETY, TOPEKA)

day. Second, the agents came armed with titles to lots in Langston City, railroad tickets to get the people there, and copies of the *Langston City Herald*. This paper sung the praises of the black town and made it seem a bustling metropolis when it had actually just begun to sprout buildings. The titles to the lots in the city provided that only blacks would own businesses or residences in the area.

People began to pour into Langston City. The Santa Fe train from Texas would pull in loaded with black migrants, mostly families with their few household goods. "It was really something to see," recalled a resident. "Some even came in wagons and lots on foot. . . . There wasn't but one building in town so most of the families lived in tents while houses were being built for them."

But Langston City was only a small part of McCabe's ambitious plans for his people in Oklahoma. He hoped to settle a black voting majority in each election district. When the territory entered the Union, McCabe planned that these voters would make Oklahoma a black state and place him in the governor's mansion. The black press of the day viewed this prospect with anticipation and enthusiasm. Here was one opportunity, as rights declined everywhere for blacks, to prove they could manage their own affairs efficiently and fairly, and without prejudice toward red or white residents.

Whites quickly decided McCabe was a formidable threat to their way of life. In February, 1890, the New York *Times* warned that a "race war" might erupt in Oklahoma and noted that McCabe had received "threats of assassination." McCabe hurried to Washington, D.C., to meet President Harrison. So did his white enemies. The Kansas City *Evening News* reported the next month: "There are a number of Oklahoma boomers of the Caucasian race now in Washington. . . . They almost foam at the mouth whenever McCabe's name is suggested for governor of Oklahoma and also at the idea of the Negroes getting control of the territory." One white was quoted as saying, "We will not tolerate Negro government here. If McCabe is appointed governor . . . I would not give five cents for his life." McCabe's response was, "If I should be appointed Governor I would administer the laws in the United States without fear or favor to white and black alike."

McCabe never made it to the governor's job, not of territory nor state of Oklahoma. He campaigned for the Republican party, heading the Logan County organization, and in 1897 was made assistant auditor for the territory. The El Reno *News* called him "undoubtedly the brainiest Negro in the territory." That same year the legislature granted forty acres for Langston College near the city McCabe founded.

The black show of political strength in many towns and McCabe's leadership hardened white opposition to black goals. By 1891 blacks had been ordered at gunpoint from several communities in the territory. Bishop Henry M. Turner, the advocate of a "back to Africa" movement, soon found a warm black response in Oklahoma. At the very moment some blacks were

Family on a claim near Guthrie, Oklahoma Territory. (WESTERN HISTORY COLLECTIONS, UNIVERSITY OF OKLAHOMA LIBRARY)

pouring into the territory, others were heeding Bishop Turner's advice and leaving for the east coast and ships that would take them to Africa. Two hundred penniless Oklahoma blacks huddled in the basement of a Methodist mission in Brooklyn, New York, waiting for the ships that would carry them to the ancestral homeland.

As Oklahoma moved toward statehood, black organizations demanded justice and equality. By 1904 major Oklahoma civil rights groups included the Suffrage League, the Equal Rights Association, the Negro Press Association, the Afro-American League, and the Negro Protective League. Black delegations were sent to Washington, D.C., to bring pressure to bear on Congress, and some met with President Theodore Roosevelt. In 1907 when Oklahoma was admitted as a state, blacks denounced the new constitution as "the most damnable instrument that was ever written, and called a constitution." Blacks held rallies in several Oklahoma cities, protesting its discriminatory features.

This was all to no avail. The first bill introduced into the Oklahoma legislature asked for segregated transportation and waiting rooms in the state. Although this law was quickly passed and quickly challenged in a lawsuit by blacks, it was not repealed until 1965.

Oklahoma was destined to become not the fulfillment of a black dream, but merely another southern nightmare. It became the first state to segregate telephone booths. It passed the grandfather clause, which kept blacks from voting because their grandfathers (who were slaves) did not vote. In Boley, a leading black town, the local paper characterized the white attitude in these words: "Not only don't they want the Negro to not vote but want him to get off the earth as well."

The black people of Oklahoma fell victim to the white supremacy they had fled. What legal tricks could not accomplish, fraud and intimidation of black voters did. Black political power was crushed in Oklahoma as elsewhere in the South. In Boley, Uncle Jesse, the town poet, sang of the lost glory of his black city:

"Oh, 'tis a pretty country
And the Negores own it, too
With not a single white man here
To tell us what to do—in Boley"

Edwin P. McCabe was beaten but not finished. Three months after Oklahoma attained statehood, he went to court to challenge the segregation of railroad passangers by race. He carried his case from one court to the next, and in the process he sold his home in Oklahoma and left the state. Perhaps he needed the money to fund his court suit, or perhaps he was in some danger in Oklahoma. Finally in 1914, the United States Supreme Court ruled in his case. It affirmed the Plessy decision that segregation was legal on Oaklahma trains and elsewhere in the United States.

McCabe and his wife moved to Chicago. He slipped into poverty and died in 1920 at age 70. His wife managed to scrape together enough money to bring McCabe's body back to Topeka, Kansas, where he had been of service to the state. he was buried in the presence of his wife, a gravedigger and a white undertaker.

Perhaps McCabe's greatest monument was in Oklahoma. Because of his efforts, 30 black towns had sprung up between 1890 and 1910 when before there were none.

SUTTON E. GRIGGS

A Black Son of Texas
Lifts His Pen

Sutton E. Griggs, born into a deeply religious Baptist home in Texas during the days of the last frontier, made his mark in the West not astride a horse or behind a six-gun, but with his powerful pen and voice. He devoted his life to the state of Texas and to achievement of pride and citizenship for his people.

In one of his many books, Griggs wrote warmly of the sturdy character of his parents. His father had a "rugged strength" and was "pre-eminently a man of peace." His mother was "loving" and "ever tender and serene of soul." A pastor in the Baptist church in Denison, Texas, Griggs's father also played an important part in the National Baptist Convention. The family was able to afford to send young Griggs to Bishop College, then in Marshall, Texas, and to Union Theological Seminary in Richmond, Virginia. He later became pastor to

Baptist churches in Virginia, Texas, and Missouri, and was known for his eloquence.

Griggs carried on a lifelong love affair with his native Texas. It rarely left his fondest thoughts, and he became the first black man to dedicate a book to a western state. His *Wisdom's Call* was dedicated to "Texas soil which fed me, to Texas air which fanned my cheeks, to Texas skies which smiled upon me, to Texas stars which searched my soul, chased out the germs of slumber."

Griggs had little time for slumber, for his other great loyalty was to his people. He grew to manhood during the era of lynch law when three or four black men (and sometimes women and children) a week were put to death by white mobs. This was also the time following Reconstruction in the South when states enacted laws disfranchising black voters and installing segregation of schools, public facilities, and southern life in general. Griggs chafed under this mounting oppression and wanted to liberate his people from its injustice.

In 1899 Griggs was twenty-six when he wrote and published his first novel, *Imperium in Imperio*. No book of the time, not even Dr. W. E. B. Du Bois's *Souls of Black Folk*, more clearly voiced black frustration and rage during the era of lynch law than this amateur novel. Young Griggs was hardly a master of his craft, and his book is a strange combination of story, anger, and Victorian morality. It is packed with silly love scenes, revolutionary talk, confrontations, and fantasies. Its characters, stiff and self-conscious, speak Griggs's viewpoints. Yet beyond the transparent characters and unbelievable plot lies a political message of great importance.

Griggs wrote as a "race patriot." At the novel's climax he urged a black revolution within the United States, though this meant bloodshed and treason. He had to publish the book himself. No review of it has ever been found, perhaps because it had too hot a subject for either black or white reviewers. Yet

Sutton E. Griggs wrote novels and lectured to help his people achieve equal rights.

Griggs's *Imperium in Imperio* was probably more widely read in the black ghettos of the day than the popular works of poet and novelist Paul Laurence Dunbar or novelist Charles W. Chesnutt. While they wrote of black life for white audiences, Griggs depicted black life for blacks.

Despite its obvious faults, the novel is remarkably modern and ahead of its time in viewpoint. Griggs describes a black-student strike at a white-run college, an event as foreign to his age as it is common to our own. In unison black students hold up signs reading "Liberty or Death" and then march out in pairs singing "the John Brown song." Griggs relates that this student strike spread to a hundred thousand young people across the country. It created "a new Negro, self-respecting, fearless, and determined in the assertion of his rights. . . ."

The title of the novel refers to a secret black government with its own President and Congress, $850,000,000 in cash, and a militant newspaper that recites the various acts of white oppression.

Griggs's two central characters clash over the use of force and violence to achieve black liberation. They debate the wisdom of revolution against the white American majority. Griggs is trying to decide whether the Imperium should become an organization like the NAACP or one like the Black Panthers. This debate takes up much of the book.

Finally, as the United States enters the Spanish-American War in 1898, the Imperium meets in Waco, Texas, to chart its course. It votes to capture Texas and Louisiana, with the aid of America's foreign enemies, and "hoist the flag of the Imperium." This plan involves giving Louisiana to the foreign allies of the Imperium. However, Griggs has reserved Texas for a Black republic. Blacks would establish a base and government in his favorite state and live out their lives unrestricted by American bigotry.

The theme of this novel is clearly black power, and its basic question is how to achieve it. Griggs also offers the concepts "Black is beautiful," "Blacks should separate from white society," and "black pride," all of which have a current ring.

Three years later Griggs published another novel. *Unfettered*, again produced by his own printing establishment in Nashville, Tennessee. He warned readers, "One day our great nation that once dealt with the Negro's woes will be summoned to deal with his strength." Griggs went on to write more novels and nonfiction works. Probably none of his books was a financial success.

He increasingly turned to church work and lecturing at Texas schools for blacks. He tried mightily to instill pride in people taught by the society around them that they were worthless. He returned to serve as pastor in his father's church in Denison, and died there in 1930.

After *Imperium in Imperio* Griggs drifted away from a radical outlook. His youthful anger developed into a driving concern to help his people and his country. He rejected the idea of violent revolt or an exodus to Africa as impractical for black Americans. Booker T. Washington rose to fame as a black leader by proposing everyone accept segregation and hope for the best. Griggs would have no part of this reasoning.

Political action to achieve equal rights was his credo. When Dr. W. E. B. Du Bois and other leaders in 1905 launched the Niagara Movement demanding immediate freedom and justice, Griggs was pleased to join them.

A passion for his people and for Texas merged in this determined Texan, who devoted his life to his home state and to enlightening and leading blacks.

Books for Further Reading

Adams, Russell L. *Great Negroes Past and Present.* (Chicago: Afro-American Press, 1964. Includes information on several prominent Californians.

Aptheker, Herbert, ed. *A Documentary History of the Negro in the United States.* New York: Citadel, 1951; reprinted, 1969.

Belous, Russell E., ed. *America's Black Heritage.* Los Angeles: Los Angeles County Museum of Natural History, 1969. A brochure with historical prints on African American people in California.

Bernard, Jacqueline. *Journey toward Freedom.* New York: W. W. Norton, 1967. The well-told story of black abolitionist Sojourner Truth, who spoke against slavery in the Midwest.

Buckmaster, Henrietta. *The Seminole Wars.* New York: Collier, 1966. About the red and black Seminoles in Florida.

Dobler, Lavinia, and Edgar A. Toppin. *Pioneers and Patriots.* New York: Zenith Books, Doubleday, Garden City, N.Y., 1965. Chapter 2 is the story of Du Sable.

Drotning, Philip T. *Black Heroes in Our Nation's History.* New York: Cowles, 1969.

——. *A Guide to Negro History in America.* Garden City, N.Y.: Doubleday, 1968. Includes references to many black settlers in its information on each western state.

Durham, Philip, and Everett L. Jones. *The Adventures of the Negro Cowboys.* New York: Dodd, Mead, 1966. The well told story for young adults of the leading Black cowhands of the last frontier.

Fairfax, Downey. *The Buffalo Soldiers in the Indian Wars.* New York: McGraw-Hill, 1969. The history of the Back Western regiments.

Felton, Howard W. *Edward Rose, Negro Trailblazer*. New York: Dodd, Mead, 1967.

———. Jim Beckwourth, *Negro Mountain Man*. New York: Dodd, Mead, 1966.

Greene, Lorenzo Johnston. *The Negro in Colonial New England*. New York: Atheneum, 1968 The only general study of early northern hlacks.

Hughes, Langston. *Famous Negro Heroes of America*. New York: Dodd, Mead, 1965.

Katz., William Loren. *The Black West: A Pictorial History*. Seattle: Open Hand Publishing, 1988. Written for adults, third edition, revised and expanded from the original 1971 edition.

———. *Black Indians: A Hidden Heritage*. New York: Atheneum Publishers, 1986. Written for young adults.

Miller, Robert. *Reflections of a Black Cowboy*. New Jersey: Silver Burdette, 1991. Two volumes of the four volumes are tales about Black cowmen.

Pelz, Ruth. *Black Heroes of the Wild West*. Seattle: Open Hand, 1989. Stories of African Americans written for little children.

Redding, Saunders. *The Lonesome Road*. Garden City, N.Y.: Doubleday, 1958.

Savage, W. Sherman. *Blacks in the West*. Westport: Greenwood Press, 1976. Based on a life-time of research into the subject.

Stewart, Paul W. and Wallace Y. Ponce. *Black Cowboys*. Broomfield: Phillips Publishing, 1986. Fascinating photos of many cowhands.

Index